□

PARTY POLITICS and PRESSURE GROUPS

A COMPARATIVE INTRODUCTION

NELSON'S POLITICAL SCIENCE LIBRARY

Editor: K. W. Watkins, Ph.D., University of Sheffield

□ Maurice Duverger □

PARTY POLITICS and PRESSURE GROUPS

A COMPARATIVE INTRODUCTION

□ translated by ROBERT WAGONER

MARITIME COLLEGE OF THE CITY UNIVERSITY
OF NEW YORK

NELSON

THOMAS NELSON AND SONS LTD
36 Park Street London W1Y 4DE
PO Box 18123 Nairobi Kenya

Thomas Nelson (Australia) Ltd
597 Little Collins Street Melbourne 3000

Thomas Nelson and Sons (Canada) Ltd
81 Curlew Drive Don Mills Ontario

Thomas Nelson (Nigeria) Ltd
PO Box 336 Apapa Lagos

Thomas Nelson and Sons (South Africa) (Proprietary) Ltd
51 Commissioner Street Johannesburg

This work was originally published as a "Partie Spéciale" in M. Duverger's
Sociologie Politique (Paris: Presses Universitaires de France, 1968).

First published in Great Britain 1972

Copyright © 1972 by Thomas Y. Crowell Company Inc.

ISBN 017 711097 X (board)
     017 712097 5 (paper)
Printed in the United States of America

□ FOREWORD □

Of all the instruments designed by man for the attainment of his political aims, perhaps none has proved so enduring as the political party. Indeed, the modern politician without his party often resembles a fish out of water. It is easy to understand this symbiosis between the professional politico and his party, for maneuver is the life of politics, and the party is a flexible machine for maneuver. And as it searches out the demands of its society, the party cannot but adapt to its culture.

Unfortunately, the very flexibility and adaptibility that so recommends the party to the politician often becomes anathema to the student of politics. There are so many different kinds of party organizations—not to mention party systems—that the student cannot help but be bewildered. The simplest strategy, that of studying parties regionally, does not satisfy, for the purely national focus does not seem to produce cumulative knowledge. However, to ignore regional differences is to slight the forces that underlie party diversity. How can this dilemma be solved?

Maurice Duverger is one of a handful of social scientists who have succeeded in combining a structural approach to party organization with a sensitive recognition of the cultural, historical, and social differences that impinge on party systems.

The beginning student who reads Duverger discovers gradually that party organizations can be categorized structurally and understood historically without doing either structure or history an injustice. Indeed, any reader will come away from this book with a surer grasp of party organizational patterns as well as with an appreciation for the national subtleties that modify these basic patterns.

Duverger also finds that interest-group structures are tied predictably to party systems. In this way, he provides the reader with a systematic, comprehensive view of the most common organizations through which man has attempted to work his will on politics. Most important, Duverger impresses the reader with the multifunctionality—and, therefore, the durability—of the party-interest group combination. Now, as these traditional political forms are being subjected to scathing attacks, this book restores our perspective.

RICHARD M. MERELMAN
Madison, Wisconsin

□ CONTENTS □

□ INTRODUCTION □

Political parties and pressure groups are the major organizations involved in the political process. There are others as well, such as the news media, but in a way, these too may be regarded as pressure groups. Political parties and pressure groups are fairly easy to differentiate, even though there are also intermediate types of organizations. For example, some parties are based on pressure groups—like the British Labour party, comprised of unions, cooperatives, and mutual aid societies; and occasionally, some pressure groups act like political parties—the *Union de Défense des Artisans et Commerçants* of Pierre Poujade, which presented candidates for the legislative elections of 1956. Two characteristics almost always set political parties apart from pressure groups: the manner in which they participate in political conflicts, and their membership base.

In the first place, political parties have as their primary goal the conquest of power or a share in its exercise. They try to win seats at elections, to name deputies and ministers, and to take control of the government. Pressure groups, on the contrary, do not seek to win power themselves, or to participate in the exercise of power; they endeavor, instead, to exert an influence on those who wield power, to bring "pressure" upon them: hence their name. Secondly, political parties draw their

1

support from a broad base, whereas pressure groups represent a limited number with a particular or private interest. By this we mean that political parties act within the framework of society as a whole, to which every individual belongs just by virtue of being a citizen, whether he accepts the basic premises of the society (conflicts *within* the regime) or challenges those premises (conflicts *over* the regime).

Pressure groups, on the other hand, act to defend their private interests. People belong to such groups as workers, as sportsmen, as opponents of the atomic bomb, as young people, as women, as Catholics, and so forth, not simply as citizens. Pressure groups thus have the nature of "corporative" organizations, in the current sense this term is given. As a matter of fact, the corporative doctrines fashionable in the 1930's advocated replacing the elected assemblies within the party framework with elected assemblies within the framework of pressure groups. The French Social and Economic Council is an assembly of this type.

However, if the concept of the political party is relatively precise, the definition of a pressure group is not. One can draw up an accurate list of political parties in any given country, but not of its pressure groups. All parties are in effect organizations specializing in political warfare, their political role being their primary or exclusive function. On the other hand, pressure groups fall into two categories: for some, the sole or primary purpose is to directly influence political power; others have an indirect and occasional influence on power, but their basic purpose and activity is essentially nonpolitical. Every association and every group can thus assume the character of a pressure group in some particular area to defend the interests it represents vis-à-vis the state (for example, a musical appreciation group seeking government subsidies for concert performances).

□ PART ONE □

POLITICAL PARTIES

Political parties developed simultaneously with electoral and parliamentary processes. They first appeared as electoral committees that procured for a candidate the sponsorship of certain prominent citizens and raised the funds necessary for the election campaign. In addition, parliamentary groups developed within legislative assemblies, uniting deputies who shared a common objective. This collaboration among deputies at the political summit naturally led to attempts to form federations of their electoral committees, and, in this manner, the first political parties were created. In the United States, the need to agree at the national level on the choice of a candidate for the presidency and then to conduct an election campaign within a vast national framework, and the need to select numerous candidates for various elective offices on the local level, gave American political parties a unique flavor and appearance. But they are, nonetheless, closely related to the question of elections.

Yet, political parties have also been adopted by political

3

regimes that have neither elections nor parliaments, and by regimes with pseudoelections and pseudoparliaments, in which a single candidate is offered to the electorate or in which a single party occupies all the seats in the legislature. We, of course, recognize these as governments with a one-party system—an expression curiously contradictory in terms, since the word "party" (from Latin *pars,* meaning "part") claims to represent the entire nation. But even in this distorted sense, the appearance of parties is linked to the development of elections and parliamentary bodies; the dictatorship uses the single party to establish the appearance of electoral and parliamentary processes and give itself a democratic façade. We must note, moreover, that the line dividing one-party regimes from multiparty regimes is not always clearly defined.

THE STRUCTURES OF POLITICAL PARTIES

In the first half of the nineteenth century, when people referred to parties, they were thinking primarily of ideologies rather than the men who subscribed to them. With Marx and Lenin, the accent was placed on the underlying social foundations: parties were viewed as the expression of social classes in a nation's political life. M. I. Ostrogorski, Roberto Michel, a number of American writers between 1920 and 1940, and the present writer have focused on structures of political parties, emphasizing in particular, their "machinery," organization, and apparatus. We have barely begun to study the image the party member has of his own party, the reason for his adherence to it, and the ties that bind him to it. Finally, recent studies on decision-making have concentrated on what the parties *do* rather than what they *are*, on their strategy rather than their organization.

Ideologies, social foundations, structure, organization, participation, strategy—all these aspects must be taken into account in making a complete analysis of any political party.

Limiting ourselves to the study of parties as organizations here does not mean we consider the other factors less important. We are simply focusing our analysis on the question of party organization, while seeking to discern its relationship to all the other elements of society that make up political parties. From this structural viewpoint, we must distinguish between the internal organization of parties and what one might call their "external" organization, that is, the relationships between the various parties of a single nation. We will call this external organization "the party system."

THE INTERNAL ORGANIZATION OF PARTIES

There is one basic distinction to be made in this connection —that between elitist or traditional parties (*partis de cadres*) and mass parties (*partis de masses*) (this distinction, which I formulated in 1951, is now generally accepted). But we must also bear in mind that there are some intermediate types that fall between the two categories, such as "indirect" parties.

ELITIST OR TRADITIONAL PARTIES

Here we must differentiate between two very different types: the European and the American.

The European Type By and large, the conservative, liberal, and radical parties of present-day Europe have retained, on the whole, the structure they acquired in the nineteenth century, and they are the prototype of the elitist party.

These parties do not aim at recruiting the largest possible membership, but at enlisting the support of notable individuals: they are more concerned with quality than with quantity. These prominent citizens are sought out either because of their prestige, which endows them with a certain moral influence, or because of their wealth, which enables them to underwrite the expenditures of election campaigns. They are grouped into local committees, corresponding to the boundaries of the various electoral districts. The internal organization of these committees is quite informal; the membership is small enough not to require a rigid organizational structure, and they operate with a large degree of autonomy. As a rule, the party's central organization has little authority or control over them. In Great Britain, however, the organization of the Liberal and Conservative parties has been more centralized than in other countries since the nineteenth century. But elsewhere, the recent tendency is also toward centralization.

With respect to the organization and function of parliamentary groups, the same characteristic distinguishes England from other nations. Everywhere, the members of Parliament play a key role; they are the true leaders of these traditional, elitist parties, even when certain militants try to challenge their authority. But in London, the members of Parliament are themselves organized in a very strict manner: discipline is imposed upon them in voting on all important issues, and the authority of the leader of the group is not questioned. Elsewhere, there is neither a disciplined vote nor a leader with unquestioned authority. We have already indicated that this difference is a critical one; it affects the very structure of political regimes. The difference between "flexible" parties (without disciplined voting) and "rigid" parties (with disciplined voting and greater centralization in general) is as important as difference between traditional parties and mass parties. Although most mass parties are rigid, and most elitist parties are flexible, Great Britain offers the example of rigid elitist parties—Conservative and Liberal.

The structure of these parties corresponds to the structure of the liberal state, which was based in the beginning on a limited or universal suffrage and where voters maintained their confidence in the traditional social elites. The system resisted the tendency to become more democratic, except for a few minor changes. The appearance of mass parties has prompted many of the elitist parties to try to emulate them; in general these attempts have failed. Despite the adoption of formal procedures for party membership, the public has tended to shy away from the older organizations; the committees of dignitaries, centered about parliamentary figures, have therefore continued to play the leading role. However, the development of campaign methods has led, in certain cases, to an increase in the number of militants at election time, notably in the door-to-door canvassing in Anglo-Saxon fashion. But these activists fall far short of the hundreds of thousands, not to say millions, of regular and permanent members that characterize socialist or communist parties.

The American Type In the United States, however, where the traditional parties have not encountered competition from mass parties, since the latter have failed to achieve any sizable development (an unusual phenomenon), a profound change has occurred in the party structures.

At the beginning of the century, the gradual establishment of a system of primary elections—a kind of pre-voting system in which citizens in general are asked to indicate the party candidates from whom they will later make a final choice at the regular election—weakened the hold of the committees of prominent citizens. In the so-called closed primaries, where voters registered in advance as Democrats or Republicans receive a ballot permitting them to designate their party's candidate, membership procedure developed that is quite different from the practice followed by European mass parties, but one that is just as real in many respects. Moreover, this hinders the establishment of mass parties, since the primary election laws forbid the candidates of the party from being designated by its members or by their delegates.

While primaries forced the party committees to open their doors to the influence of the general voting public, campaign requirements led the American parties to set up a highly developed system of permanent party organization, beginning at the level of small electoral districts (the precincts, encompassing from 400 to 500 voters). At the head of each precinct, a party member of demonstrated loyalty, the captain, provides regular contact between the party hierarchy and the voters, not just at election time. Moreover, the nature and function of precinct captains seems to be changing. Formerly, they acted mainly to provide certain small favors or services, developing ties with the voters that were based on material interests and a kind of businesslike reciprocity, rather than on a party loyalty. But party loyalty seems to be acquiring added importance in recent years, while, at the same time, the captain's functions are being increasingly taken over by women concerned with civic action.

This dual process has not transformed American parties into mass parties. They retain a hierarchical structure in which the main directives emanate from committees of party professionals who are not chosen democratically. But they have established closer and more regular contact with the voting public than have the traditional European parties. And they have developed a much stronger framework, a much firmer organization: the captains follow the directives of the local committee very strictly. However, this discipline does not extend to the top of the political hierarchy; although very powerful at the local level, it is weaker on the state level, and practically nonexistent at the national level. Above all, American political parties have never been able to—or wanted to—establish a disciplined vote among their legislative groups in Congress. They remain flexible parties, in the sense in which we have defined this term.

MASS PARTIES

The technique of organizing mass parties was invented more than a half-century ago by the socialist movements, and was later adopted by communist parties, fascist parties, and, more recently, by parties in underdeveloped countries. Certain Christian-Democratic parties are also mass parties, while others —like the French MRP (Popular Republican Movement)— remain traditional parties. But, as a rule, there is nothing unique about their structure since they were patterned after the socialist parties.

The Socialist Type At the outset, the mass party technique was developed to finance the elections of worker candidates, who were regarded at the time as revolutionaries and could not, therefore, hope to gain the financial support of bankers, industrialists, businessmen, or large landowners—the groups that underwrote the campaign expenses of liberal and conservative candidates.

In Great Britain, campaign financing by trade unions and cooperatives resulted in the formation of indirect parties. In Germany, where the unions were weaker, and in France, where they were more suspicious of political action, such a structure was inconceivable. The idea was then developed of enrolling as many members as possible in the party on a permanent basis, and having each one pay a regular annual, or even a monthly, assessment that would nourish the campaign coffers. Since they could not finance the party through large contributions from prominent citizens—as the traditional parties did—they would provide for its sustenance with small, regular dues paid for by ordinary citizens.

The financial question was, of course, not the only important issue. Because they did not want the party's candidates chosen by the inner circle of a small committee, a democratic representation of the membership was organized, within local or national party congresses, to select the candidates and direct party policies (an objective similar to that of the American primaries but one achieved by different means). At the same time, regular meetings of various sections of the party took on the appearance of political "night school," designed to pro-

Perhaps a reason for the 'essentiality' of parties? To educate an unwise the electorate in the governing process? Could this not equally be achieved by a no of interest grps?

vide civic education for the electorate and help them to exercise their legal rights fully.

There seems to be a rather close correlation between this new type of party and the evolution of its social foundation. The traditional hierarchies corresponded to the conflict between the aristocracy and the bourgeoisie—social classes whose numbers were small, so they could be adequately represented by a few prominent individuals. The narrowness of the parties reflected the narrowness of the political field and the profound nature of a democracy from which the majority of the people were virtually excluded from representation. On the other hand, the mass parties corresponded to the expansion of democracy, encompassing almost the entire population. The people cannot truly exercise their rights if they limit themselves to casting a vote every four or five years; they must really participate, on a regular basis, in the affairs of government, and they can do so through the new organization of political parties.

This point is questioned don't they participate more through p grps than through the party structure

The permanent enlistment of hundreds of thousands, even millions, of people (since 1913 the German Social Democratic party has had more than a million members), the regular payment of a kind of party tax, which is what dues are, required a much more rigid administrative organization than we find in the traditional parties. This accounts for the gradual development of a complex, hierarchical party apparatus and the formation of a central committee of "internal leaders," which weakens the position of those holding parliamentary offices. In the traditional parties, the elected deputies directed party policies with no serious challenge to their authority. But the revolutionary doctrine of the socialist parties naturally led them to distrust the parliamentary atmosphere and to be fearful of its corrupting influence on the deputies of the working class: hence the principle of strict subordination of the deputies to the central committee elected by party militants.

From a sociological standpoint, the conflict between two

groups of leaders is interesting because it reflects the struggle between two underlying communities: the party members who elect internal party leaders and the voters who elect parliamentary deputies. Party members, who are more "partisan" than ordinary voters, are clearly more intransigent in their positions. But the evolution of socialist parties in the direction of social democracy and their progressive integration into the parliamentary system have altered the situation. In accepting parliamentary principles, the socialists were naturally prompted to attach primary importance to those who embody them: the deputies. On the other hand, in communist or fascist parties, where these principles are not always accepted, the members of parliaments remain subservient to the dictates of their party's central committee, which consequently holds greater influence and prestige.

The Communist Type The first Western communist parties, born of schisms within the socialist parties, were patterned after the socialists. But a decision by the Comintern in 1924 forced them to adopt the organization of the Soviet Communist party. Strongly influenced by the need for clandestine action, imposed on the Bolsheviks before 1917, these party structures have proven to be very effective in maintaining an organization that is both flexible and unified for large masses of people. Communist parties are the best organized of all parties; this technical factor must not be overlooked in explaining their success.

The first unique feature of the communist parties is its basic element—the cell. Like the socialist parties, and unlike the traditional parties, communist parties try to attract a very large membership. But they do not organize in the same way at the local level. Instead of grouping their members according to place of residence, communist parties organize them by place of work. Instead of local committees and districts, they set up "work cells" in factories, shops, stores, schools, and the like, which has a twofold advantage. First, contact between

the members of the basic community is closer and more frequent, since they see one another daily at work, and they can
also receive daily party directives and take joint action. Second,
the problems of their work or business enterprise furnish material for discussion within the cell. By linking these matters
to general party policies, the latter acquire a tangible reality.
Each member becomes keenly aware of the importance and
meaning of his party membership. Feelings of solidarity regarding one's work are stronger than those regarding one's
neighborhood or community; hence they draw the party members within a cell much closer together. Of course, alongside
the cells established in business enterprises, there are local
cells of communist parties (rural cells, and cells uniting isolated workers), but these, to some extent, have a residual
character. Even when they are more numerous than the cells
existing in factories and businesses, the latter are considered to
be more important.

Another characteristic differentiates the communist cell from
a socialist cell; generally it is a much smaller community. A
socialist section may include several hundred, even several
thousand, members (in the cities); the communist cell, on the
contrary, normally includes only a few dozen members. When
a cell is too large, it is subdivided as soon as a capable secretary
can be found for the new cell. Solidarity is obviously stronger
within a small homogeneous group than within a larger, more
heterogeneous group.

Communist parties are organized in an authoritarian and
centralized manner. To be sure, the leaders are formally
elected, but the elections are simply acts of ratification, as in
most parties. Actually, the central committee plays the main
role in selecting leaders. Decisions are taken by the central committee, and local leaders have the task of executing its decisions.
Power descends from the top down; it does not move upward.
However, communists describe this centralism as "democratic"
because discussions, as broadly based as possible, are required
at all levels before a decision is reached. These discussions are

held for the purpose of informing the central committee, which must take all views into account and not lose contact with the party's foundation. In truth, the debates and discussions on the cell level are genuine. During the Stalinist era, they gradually thinned out as one moved up the pyramid of authority, to disappear altogether at the top. It is by no means certain that these practices have been entirely abandoned today; certain differences are noticeable among the various communist parties.

Lastly, we must not overlook the crucial role of party doctrine within the communist parties. Of course, all parties are more or less wedded to some ideology, even fascist parties which pretend otherwise, but in no other party does ideology play such an important role. In no other party is ideology so closely tied to political action or is there such concern with giving its members theoretical indoctrination. No other party goes to such lengths to explain its practical strategy in terms of doctrinal principles or gives such prominence to ideological discussions. These discussions are inevitably marked by a certain amount of pedantry or scholasticism, which can be quite ponderous and wearisome. Indeed, the exegeses of Marxist writers sometimes resemble theological disputations of the Middle Ages. Every cultural system contains defects of this kind, especially when it begins to acquire a certain rigidity. Sociologists recognize that Marxism is a cultural system, and, as such, its organizational structure is broader and deeper than that of any other party.

The Fascist Type It has often been said of fascist parties that they try to imitate communist techniques. Mussolini himself frequently made this claim, and modern theoreticians of "psychological warfare," who attribute their inspiration to Mao Tse-tung, are following a well-traveled road. However, we must not exaggerate these ties or resemblances. Fascist parties have a rigid structure, a high degree of centralization, and a vertical line of authority. But many other organizations and parties present similar characteristics, not merely the communists. Fascism borrowed from communism the idea of a single party, but it applied the idea in a very different fashion. Actually, the internal structures of the two are quite dissimilar.

A unique feature of fascist parties is the application of military techniques to a mass political organization. To be sure, all of their members do not belong to militias or assault platoons, but these comprise the backbone of the party, with the others providing a kind of "reserve" for those "on active duty." The basic unit is thus a very small group, about a dozen men, easy to assemble at any given moment because of their proximity (the same street or apartment building). These small groups are linked to each other in a hierarchical chain of command, as in the army. Thus, in a Nazi assault platoon, there was the squad (*Schar*), consisting of four to twelve men; the platoon (*Truppe*), consisting of three to six squads; the company (*Sturm*), consisting of four platoons; the battalion (*Sturmbann*), consisting of two companies; the regiment (*Standarte*), consisting of three to five battalions; the brigade (*Untergruppe*), consisting of three regiments; and last, the division (*Gruppe*), consisting of four to seven brigades. Hence, depending upon requirements, various sizes of troop units were available for combat.

Fascist political combat is also military in nature. Members of fascist militias undergo training similar to that of soldiers, learning to wear a uniform, salute, march in formation, handle weapons, and engage in military combat. They are taught sabotage, how to break up meetings, how to fight other saboteurs, how to seize control of a party or union headquarters, how to "rough up" their opponents, and how to conduct street fighting. A fascist party is essentially a kind of private army with which one seeks to seize power by force and to hold it in the same manner. This type of organization is related to fascist doctrine, which draws a sharp line between elite groups and the masses, granting to the former a natural right to command the latter. In order to exercise this right, the force of arms must offset the force of numbers.

The organization of fascist parties reflects their social basis. Fascism has developed thus far in two types of societies: (1) in a highly developed technological society (Germany in 1933), where economic crisis made the affluent bourgeoisie and the middle classes afraid of the establishment of a communist or socialist regime, and (2) in older, less technologically advanced societies (Spain and Portugal), where a feudal, agrarian aristocracy feared a movement toward democracy. Italy represents an intermediate situation; in the north it is more like Germany, and in the south more like Spain and Portugal. In both cases, a privileged minority dreads being pushed by the majority in undesired political directions. Against mounting pressure from the majority, its only effective means of defense is violence. As the social and doctrinal basis of fascism, it is not surprising that violence is reflected in its party organization. Of course, this does not prevent fascist parties from also having recourse to propaganda techniques or from seeking to use elections and parliamentary processes to attain positions of power (indeed, the Nazis began to acquire power following an election victory and by engaging in "cloakroom politics"). But violence remains the principal weapon of fascism.

THE INTERMEDIATE TYPES

Two kinds of intermediate organizations stand between the mass parties and the elitist—indirect parties and the parties in underdeveloped countries, both of which are closer to mass parties than to the traditional parties.

Indirect Parties The British Labour party in its original organization of 1900 exemplifies this type of party. At that time, it did not recruit a regular party membership. Its main committees were formed by union representatives, mutual aid societies, cooperatives, and intellectual groups (for example, the Fabian Society), who agreed to take common action on political issues. These committees chose candidates for elections and controlled the campaign funds established for this purpose by contributions from each group.

The Labour party system was more or less adopted by socialist parties in Scandinavia and Belgium before 1940. It could also be found in the Christian-Democratic parties in Belgium and Austria between 1919 and 1936, which were established on a corporative basis in which party committees were formed from delegates of trade unions, farm organizations, middle-class associations, and so on. Basically, it was an adaptation of the procedures followed by the traditional parties of the nineteenth century; instead of having distinguished citizens selected because of their titles or wealth, the committees were made up of "functioning" dignitaries, official representatives of the various organizations.

The representatives themselves bring together a very large group of members, thus including the general populace in the system, but only in an indirect manner. They do not belong to the party itself: they belong to an organization that is a collective member of the party—which is not the same thing as individual membership. Legal reforms, enacted in Great Britain in 1927 and 1945, demonstrated, however, that only one-third of the membership in the trade unions would refuse to join the Labour party on a personal basis if an individual, written commitment were required, similar to the one demanded for membership in the communist or socialist parties. Therefore, this system is clearly an intermediate type between mass parties and traditional parties.

Parties in Underdeveloped Countries The great new development of the past ten years or so has been the appearance and growth of political parties in underdeveloped countries. In some instances, they are not fundamentally different from parties in Western Europe, the Soviet Union, or North America. The Communist party in China or Vietnam, for example, is not basically different from the Soviet Communist party, despite numerous distinct features. A number of conservative and liberal parties bear an odd resemblance to traditional European parties of the nineteenth century, being based on a few prominent individuals. But on the other hand, certain parties, like those in Black Africa, have a pronounced originality, seeming to represent a particular type, one that is closer to mass parties than to traditional parties.

In all mass parties, the leaders form a group quite distinct from the rest of the membership and from the party militants: this "inner circle" resembles somewhat the leadership of the traditional parties submerged, as it were, in the heart of a mass organization. However, the line separating the two groups is not rigid in technologically advanced societies; the inner circle remains quite open, and the rank-and-file member can gain admission rather easily. The distinction is based more upon technical requirements (the need to concentrate power for political effectiveness) rather than on a sociological situation. But in underdeveloped countries, on the contrary, in the mass parties, the social distance between members of the "inner circle" and all the others is very great. The former have reached the intellectual and technological level of modern societies, while the others still remain much closer to the level of primitive societies. Thus the structure of the political parties reflects the general structure of the countries themselves at their current stage of development.

PARTY SYSTEMS

In every country, over a relatively long period of time, there is a certain stability in the number of parties, their internal structures, their ideologies, even their respective sizes, alliances, and types of opposition. Therefore, we can describe the "party system" of any country during a given period of time. A comparative study of the various party systems reveals certain marked similarities among certain ones; thus we may describe the kinds of systems which appear to have a profound influence on the structure and functioning of political regimes. The classification generally adopted in this connection distinguishes pluralistic party systems from one-party systems. But the notion of a "dominant party" serves as a kind of bridge between pluralistic and one-party systems.

PLURALISTIC PARTY SYSTEMS

In a pluralistic party system, at least two parties coexist, with no single one enjoying an overwhelming and constant superiority over the other (or others); if one does predominate, it then becomes a "dominant party" system. Within the pluralistic systems today, a basic distinction is recognized between a two-party system and a multiparty system, based upon functional differences in democratic institutions.

The distinction between a two-party and a multiparty system is therefore very important, but the importance must not be exaggerated. For the formation of regular party alliances—entering election battles with specific programs mutually agreed upon, and cooperating thereafter in their enactment—makes a multiparty system resemble a two-party system. Conversely, when each party is extremely flexible, when there is no disciplined voting in parliament, governmental majorities become shaky and unstable, and a two-party system resembles a multiparty system. A "flexible two-party system" is really much closer to a multiparty system than to the "rigid two-party system" of the British type.

Multiparty Systems The number of parties, the size of each, their structure, and their organization must all be considered simultaneously. Contrary to popular opinion, for instance, the uniqueness of the French party system lies not in the great number of parties but rather in the weakness of their organization, especially among the right-wing and center parties. With five or six main parties, France is not very different from most other Western European countries. But the lack of party discipline in France, and the feeble hold the parties have on the majority of the population, is a more significant variation.

From the standpoint of numbers, the types of multiparty systems are theoretically unlimited, but practically speaking, the situation is much simpler. Actually, there are three main categories of multiparty systems: countries such as Belgium and Austria, with a three-party system; countries—France, Italy, and northern Europe, for example—with four to six parties, to which a few small parliamentary groups are sometimes added, artificially increasing the figure; and finally, countries such as Republican Spain and Austria before 1914, with a very large number of parties. This last type seems to reflect the addition of ethnic or regional divisions to political divisions. The three-party type sometimes indicates a transitional stage between two two-party systems, as was the case in Great Britain between 1920 and 1935, a changeover period between the disappearance of the Conservative-Liberal system and the emergence of the Conservative-Labour system.

Alliances can often change the complexion of a multiparty system. If two large permanent coalitions are formed, offering the electorate a common legislative program and acting in concert in parliament, it is very much like a two-party system. Beneath the surface appearance of a multiparty system, there is really a kind of deeply imbedded two-party system. But, of course, everything depends on the solidarity of the alliances and on the discipline within the coalition parties. One must always be wary of legalistic definitions and look for the sociological reality behind external appearances. The dual nature of Dutch coalitions between 1868 and 1925 was more rigid than the present two-party system in America. The alliance in Australia between the conservative and rural parties produced a more stable parliamentary majority than that enjoyed by the president of the United States.

Again we are confronted with the problem of internal party structures. The parties within a given country do not necessarily have the same kind of structure. On the contrary, in most European nations and those of the British Commonwealth, a diversity of structures is the rule. In general, the conservative, liberal, and radical parties have retained the party structures of the nineteenth century; socialist parties, on the other hand, are mass or indirect parties (Great Britain); communist parties are also mass parties, but are organized somewhat differently from the socialist parties. Finally, there is a greater structural resemblance between parties of the same type in different countries than between the various parties within the same country—between the communist parties of two different countries, for example, than between a communist and conservative party within the same country.

Nevertheless, it is still possible to describe each country's party system in terms of its structure; a country's parties are colored by certain common characteristics, despite their differences. In France, for example, the weakness of party organization is obvious if we compare each party with its counterpart in other countries. Although the French Socialist party is more strongly organized than the British or Scandinavian conservative parties, it is weaker than the socialist party organization in England or Scandinavia; and, further, the French parties of the right have weaker organizations than the right-wing parties in the rest of Europe. The respective average size of each party, over a certain period of time, also has important consequences. In France, from 1945 to 1947, the rigidity of the party system was a result of the fact that three highly organized, well-disciplined parties accounted for more than 75 per cent of the parliamentary seats (Communists, Socialists, and members of the MRP. After the Communists were excluded from the majority in 1947, the system became somewhat more flexible. This was followed by an electoral decrease in the MRP and in the SFIO [*Section Française de l'Internationale Ouvrière:* the French Socialist party], which, together with the decreased parliamentary representation of the Communist party, brought about a return to the flexible party system, not unlike that of the Third Republic [1870–1940].

Two-Party Systems Obviously, there are fewer types of two-party systems, simply in terms of mathematical possibilities. Although the number of parties is not a factor here, the existence of very small political groups may sometimes affect the system if one happens to be in a position to shift the balance between the two major parties when each holds approximately the same number of seats. Certain independent senators in Washington have occupied this position, but it is not an especially crucial one there because of the great flexibility of the two major American parties. But at the end of the nineteenth and the beginning of the twentieth century, the Irish derived a great advantage from a similar situation in Great Britain. In a two-party system, alliances are excluded in principle, since the result would be a disguised form of the single-party system. Nevertheless, these occasionally occur in time of war (the Sacred Union or the National Union of Portugal), and in the United States, there have been alliances on certain issues, like foreign policy, temporarily removed from the domain of political controversy (*bipartisanship*).

The relative size of political parties enables us to establish a typology that is not quite so vague. There are three principal situations. First, the two parties may be almost equal in size over a fairly long period of time, in which case a very slight shift in the electorate can alter the majority, which depends for victory on a small number of "marginal" votes. This means that governmental power may be transferred from one major party to the other at rather frequent intervals. Second, if the two parties are not similar in size, and one has a substantially greater following than the other, then the larger party is assured of being in power for a prolonged period of time, during which a slow process of erosion gradually weakens its hold and enables the opposition party to come to power.

In this case, changes in government occur infrequently. Finally, there is the situation in which the differential in size is so great that the smaller party has virtually no hope of attaining power except over a very long period of time. At this point we are closer to the "dominant party system" than to a genuine two-party system.

The distinction between pseudo and genuine two-party systems is of secondary importance. The main difference involves the degree of party discipline. In the British Parliament, for example, each of the two parties forms a homogeneous group in which all the deputies vote the same way on issues of political importance. Anyone disregarding party directives is excluded from membership. This discipline in parliamentary voting is the main factor insuring the stability and authority of the government. The prime minister, who is the leader of the majority party, can count on the obedience of the members of his majority; he can be certain that this majority will support him throughout the entire legislative session, at the risk of creating a crisis within the party whose first effect would be to remove the party from power at the next general election. In the American Congress, on the other hand, each senator or representative votes according to his personal preferences without consulting his party. Hence the line separating the majority party from the opposition is not the same as the line separating Democrats from Republicans. Actually, there is a different majority and a different opposition for each issue, and it does not follow party lines. The "flexible two-party system" of the American variety is closer to a multiparty system than to a "rigid two-party system" of the British type, when viewed in terms of its political results.

FACTORS IN A TWO-PARTY AND A MULTIPARTY SYSTEM

Why do Britain and the United States have only two parties; Belgium and Australia, three; the Scandinavian countries, four or five; France and Italy, six to nine, and so forth? Many explanations have been offered, but none is wholly satisfactory. The party system existing in a given country, at a given moment, appears to be the result of many complex factors, none of which can be considered without reference to the others.

Socioeconomic Factors Political parties mirror social classes or other kinds of social groups (ethnic, ideological, religious), so socioeconomic factors are clearly the most significant ones in determining political structure. The development of political parties, in conjunction with the social structures and the ideologies expressing them, is a subject we will examine later in greater detail. For the moment we shall limit ourselves to a few general observations.

The evolutionary course of European political parties during the past 150 years has produced three basic tendencies— conservative, liberal, and socialist—which are reflected in two great succeeding conflicts, which is to say, two essentially two-party situations. In the nineteenth century, the struggle between the conservative and liberal parties represented a class conflict between the aristocracy and the bourgeoisie, a good description of which is found in the Marxist analysis. The tendency toward a two-party system was clearly evident. In the second half of the century, industrial growth and an ever larger working class resulted in the formation of a third politico-social force embodied in the socialist parties. The earlier two-party system then tended to become a three-party system, a phenomenon that appeared in its present form in Britain, Belgium, and Australia. Elsewhere, other factors intervened, but its presence remained clearly discernible.

Meanwhile, the growth of the socialist parties confronted the liberal parties with the dilemma of having to choose between two alternatives. The various liberal parties were united in their opposition to monarchies and aristocracies and in their attachment to the ideals of liberty and political equality. But liberals always defend free enterprise and private ownership of the means of production, which socialists would like to see abolished. The first party positions, mentioned above, encouraged the liberals to unite with the socialists against the conservatives; while the latter positions tended to draw the liberals closer to the conservatives and separate them from the socialists. In the first phase of political change, when the old political regimes were still well entrenched and domination by the aristocracy seemed the most serious and imminent threat, and when the weakness of the socialist parties made them seem to pose little danger to the bourgeoisie, the liberal parties usually adopted the first strategy, that of supporting the socialists. But as political democracy was gradually established and became the accepted way of life, and as the prospect of a return to the unwanted aristocratic system became more and more unlikely, the political hostility between conservatives and liberals eventually lost any real foundation. It was then natural for them to draw together in a common desire to defend private property and the established social order (the liberal order, that is, to which the conservatives rallied for lack of any choice in the matter).

Thus we witness a fusion tendency among conservatives and liberals in the direction of forming a single party opposed to the socialists. A "twentieth-century two-party system" is consequently tending to replace the "nineteenth-century two-party system." This movement is clearly observable in Great Britain, New Zealand, and Australia. In other countries, a liberal party has managed to survive, greatly diminished in size, with most of its former members having joined the conservatives. Such is the case in Belgium, the Netherlands, Scandinavia, and France (where it is called the "Radical party"). Often these small liberal parties try to play a tactical role of tipping the scales one way or the other, sometimes allied with the socialists against the conservatives, at other times allied with the conservatives against the socialists. This latter alliance has become progressively more common than the former.

In certain countries, national conflicts have complicated this general outline: systems that were basically two-party have become multiparty. In the Netherlands, for example, religious differences have interfered with political alignments. The conservative tendency was divided from the outset into the Catholic conservatives and the Protestant conservatives ("anti-revolutionaries"), and a schism among the latter led to the "historical Christians," resulting finally in three distinct conservative parties. In France, the political regimes and the conflicts they provoked have brought about a similar division among the forces of the political right. Beginning in the second half of the nineteenth century, the conservatives divided into three parties (*légitimistes, orléanistes,* and *bonapartistes*), and this fragmentation is partly responsible for the absence of any well-organized party on the right, a characteristic of the French party system. In other countries, ethnic or regional opposition groups have played a similar role and contributed to the proliferation of political parties.

The Russian Revolution of 1917 posed a great problem for the socialist parties, when the majority of them refused to rally to the Third Internationale, directed by Moscow. As a result, party splits were produced almost everywhere, giving birth to a number of communist parties. The latter have remained weak in Scandinavia, Belgium, the Netherlands, Great Britain, and the British Commonwealth; the existing party systems have scarcely been affected by their presence. On the other hand, the communist parties became powerful in Germany (from 1919 to 1933), in France, in Italy (since 1945), and in Finland; in these countries, the number of parties has consequently increased, and the multiparty system has been intensified. The development of fascism in Italy and Germany produced similar phenomena within the right-wing parties; in most European countries, parties with fascist tendencies have remained very small groups of little importance; in a few countries, however, they have given rise to important political organizations (even after World War II): Poujadism in France and neo-fascism in Italy.

The Technical Factor: The Electoral System To these socio-economic and historical factors a technical factor must be added: the electoral system. I expressed its effects in 1946 in the formulation of three sociological laws: (1) a majority vote on one ballot is conducive to a two-party system; (2) proportional representation is conducive to a multiparty system; (3) a majority vote on two ballots is conducive to a multiparty system, inclined toward forming coalitions.

The brutal finality of a majority vote on a single ballot forces parties with similar tendencies to regroup their forces at the risk of being overwhelmingly defeated. Let us assume an election district in which 100,000 voters with moderate views are opposed by 80,000 communist voters. If the moderates are divided into two parties, the communist candidate may well win the election; should one of his opponents receive more than 20,000 votes, the other will be left with less than 80,000, thereby insuring the election of the communist. In the following election, the two parties with moderate views will naturally tend to unite. Should they fail to do so, the weaker party would gradually be eliminated as a dual consequence of "under-representation" and "polarization." Under-representation is a mechanical phenomenon. Elections determined by a majority vote on one ballot literally pulverize third parties (and would do worse to fourth or fifth parties, if there were any; but none exist for this very reason). Even when a single ballot system operates with only two parties, the one that wins is favored, and the other suffers. The first one is over-represented—its proportion of seats is greater than its percentage of the votes—while the party that finishes second is usually under-represented—its proportion of seats is smaller than its percentage of the votes. The English, with their two-party system, have expressed this phenomenon by the law of the cube: the relationship in the percentage of seats held by the two parties would be equal to the relationship of the cubes of the percentages of the votes received (if a and b are the percentages of the votes, and a' and b' the percentages of the seats, then we find that $\dfrac{a'}{b'} = \dfrac{a^3}{b^3}$. When there is a third party, it is even more under-represented than the second. The gap is generally quite large, with the proportion of seats far below the proportion of the votes received. In 1964, the British Liberal party received 11.2 per cent of the votes cast, but only 1.4 per cent of the parliamentary seats. This under-representation tends to eliminate the effects of any votes cast for a third party. But voters are aware of this phenomenon. They also know that a division of votes between two parties holding similar views favors their common adversary. In the case mentioned before, the moderate voters would see clearly that a split between the moderate candidates guarantees a Communist victory: in a subsequent election they would drop the weaker of the two moderate candidates. Thus it is that voters tend to abandon the third party in order to concentrate their votes on the two strongest parties. This tendency toward polarization, a psychological phenomenon, strengthens the mechanical factors conducive to a two-party system.

In a system of proportional representation, the situation is quite different. The very principle of proportional representation explains the multiplicity of parties it produces. Since every minority, no matter how weak it may be, is assured of representation in the legislature, nothing prevents the formation of splinter parties, often separated only by mere shades of opinion. If the conservative party has 6 million votes in the country, corresponding to 300 seats in parliament, and if it splits into three groups about equal in numbers, proportional representation will give each of these about a hundred deputies, and the conservative family will have the same strength in parliament. In other respects, this electoral system does not encourage parties to unite. A coalition is useless from an electoral point of view since the entire system tends to permit everyone to take his chances at the polls. Hence the reciprocal independence of the political parties.

In a system in which elections are decided by a majority vote on the second of two ballots, political parties are numerous because the existence of a second ballot permits each party to test its chances on the first one without risking irrevocable defeat through the splintering of parties holding similar views; the regrouping occurs on the second ballot through the game of "withdrawals." Let us again use the illustration of an election district in which the conservatives have 100,000 voters and the communists, 80,000. If the conservative electorate divides into two parties, with the first receiving 60,000 votes and the second, 40,000, while the communists vote as a bloc on the first ballot, there will still be a second ballot. For the second round, the weaker conservative candidate will withdraw. His supporters will switch their votes to the stronger candidate, who will normally be elected. New parties can thus multiply, but they are usually driven to form alliances with one another to check their opponents by means of "retreats" and "withdrawals." The second ballot is essentially a voting by coalitions, as was seen in France during the Third Republic and in Imperial Germany, the two large countries that have practiced this system.

Although the preceding laws have been much discussed, often in heated debate, they have never been seriously challenged. The criticism directed against them has not questioned the reality of the phenomenon they express, which is fairly obvious, as much as the precise extent of its influence. It is clear that an electoral reform by itself will not create new parties: parties are a reflection of social forces; they are not born of a simple legislative decision. We can be sure that the relationship between electoral systems and party systems is not something mechanical and automatic. A given electoral regime does not necessarily produce a given party system; it simply exerts an influence in the direction of a particular type of system; it is a force, acting in the midst of other forces, some of which move in an opposite direction. It is also clear that the relationship between electoral and party systems is not a one-way phenomenon; if a one-ballot vote tends toward a two-party system, a two-party system also favors the adoption of a single ballot voting system.

The exact role of the electoral system seems, in the last analysis, to be that of an accelerator or that of a brake. An election by a majority vote on a single ballot has a dual effect: first, it poses an obstacle to the appearance of a new party, although this obstacle is not insurmountable (the role of a brake); secondly, it tends to eliminate the weakest party (or parties) if there are more than two (the role of an accelerator). The braking effect was noticeable in Great Britain at the end of the nineteenth century, in the face of a socialist drive, and again after World War I, in the face of communist and fascist movements. The accelerating effect was even more apparent in the case of the Liberal party, which was practically eliminated in fifteen years (1920–35), although it retains a certain number of supporters who are compelled by the electoral system to choose between Conservatives and Labourites. Deciding by a majority vote on one ballot accelerated in Great Britain the substitution of a two-party system for any other kind.

Proportional representation plays just the opposite role. It does not slow down the development of new parties. It passively registers their appearance, sometimes amplifying the vibrations they generate, like an echo chamber or a seismograph. (In order to check this tendency, proportional representation is rarely applied *in toto;* it is modified by such measures as permitting local districts to apportion residual votes and by establishing rules regarding the percentage of votes required to gain representation in the legislative assembly.) On the other hand, it retards the elimination of old parties which would otherwise tend to disappear as the social and political scene changes. The "salvaging" of the Belgian Liberal party through proportional representation, beginning in 1900, is a typical example of this phenomenon. Instead of giving way to a twentieth-century-style two-party system, the nineteenth-century system survived with the new system superimposed on it, producing an essentially three-party system (this was also the case in Germany and Austria). However, we must of course distinguish between old movements, deeply rooted among a portion of the population, and superficial movements reflecting temporary political moods or fashions. Proportional representation registers just as clearly the appearance as it does the disappearance of parties of this latter type. Typical examples were the case of "rexism" in Belgium, and, in France, the RPF [*Rassemblement du Peuple Français*] in 1951, and Poujadism in 1956.

The results of the two-ballot majority system are similar to those of proportional representation, with a few differences. The two-ballot system seems to be more discouraging to the formation of new parties than proportional representation (but it is far less effective in this than the single-ballot majority vote). Perhaps it is also more helpful to older parties, but it is difficult to formulate any definite conclusions in this matter. Furthermore, it seems to present a certain barrier to brusque changes of political opinion, to movements reflecting momentary moods or impulses, to political groups that are "fashionable" but ephemeral (even though the example of the UNR [*Union Nouvelle pour la République*, the Gaullist party] in 1958 proved to be of a different kind: but the circumstances in this instance were very special). The sharpest difference with the system of proportional representation concerns electoral alliances. A coalition system par excellence, the two-ballot regime can sometimes permit the formation of a dual system of alliances, introducing a sort of two-party system in the midst of a multi-party situation. This phenomenon was quite evident in France during the Third and the Fifth Republics, and in Germany from 1870 to 1914.

Having said all this, the fact remains that a change in the electoral system does not always have a decisive influence on the existing party system. However, it seems certain that if proportional representation were to replace the majority vote in Great Britain, a three-party system would appear before very long, making party splits within the ranks of the Labourites and the Conservatives much more likely. The influence of a one-ballot vote in maintaining an already established two-party system is beyond question. It is much less certain that the adoption of such an electoral system would destroy an already existing multiparty system and, for example, reduce to two the number of parties in France or Italy. In any event, a reform of this nature is inconceivable, because an election determined by a majority vote on a single ballot gives rise to unforeseen results when more than two parties are involved. Yet in the German Federal Republic and in Austria, such an electoral reform would very likely hasten the trend, already underway, toward a two-party system. Above all, it would prevent any move in the opposite direction by posing a serious obstacle to possible splits within the two major parties, and would also discourage the revival of small political parties.

A ONE-PARTY SYSTEM AND A DOMINANT PARTY SYSTEM

The expression "one-party system" seems to have been invented by the theorists of fascism and has been in common usage since the 1930's. The term "dominant party system," on the contrary, is a recent one. First coined in 1951, it has just begun to enter everyday language. Moreover, the current tendency is to use it in a more restricted sense than when it was first adopted—the dominant party system being a kind of intermediate type between a pluralistic system and a one-party system.

One-Party Systems The principal works dedicated to the study of one-party systems are those by fascist authors, such as M. Manoïlesco and Marcel Déat. They place great emphasis on the similarity between the single-party fascist regimes and the single-party communist regimes. This is a curious attitude, revealing a certain inferiority complex. It is noteworthy that communist writers, on the other hand, violently reject any such comparison. In practice, however, the confusion is frequently made. In the West, there is a tendency to regard the one-party system as a homogeneous type, within which internal differences are relatively minor. This view is only one aspect of a general attitude toward dictatorships, which appears in this age in the one-party system. Because Western thought considers dictatorships as an absolute evil, it has neglected their study; it examines and judges them *en bloc,* without analyzing them in detail. However, very great differences separate dictatorial regimes in general and one-party political systems in particular. The single-party situation, its ideology, and its importance in the state vary widely from one country to another.

□ INTERNAL STRUCTURE Since the majority of one-party regimes existing prior to World War II were either fascist or communist, there is a tendency to believe that the structures of fascist or communist parties are inherent in the system. However, Kemalism [in Turkey] was already creating a different image of a one-party system. The Republican Party of the People of Turkey was organized more like a traditional party than a mass party. A number of different trends were evident and various factions clashed with one another. It was closer in structure to the French Radical-Socialist party than to a fascist or communist party. And, in Portugal, Salazar's National Union party more nearly resembled a nineteenth-century conservative party than a fascist organization. The contemporary development of one-party systems in newly independent nations has shown that they can accommodate themselves to a wide variety of structures. Certain characteristics of the Neo-Destour party organization in Tunisia resemble those of communist parties, others resemble those of socialist parties, while still others recall the mass parties in underdeveloped countries.

☐ POLITICAL ORIENTATION Of still greater importance are differences in ideology and political significance. As is the case with all dictatorships, those built on a one-party system can have one of two diametrically opposed objectives. These regimes of violence appear in times of great crisis or of rapid change in social structures. Their aim could be to hasten the change and resolve the crisis by replacing the old power balance with a new one, or to attempt to prevent the change and restore the traditional social order, at the cost of a few minor changes that do not affect basic conditions. Hence, dictatorships can be either revolutionary or conservative. The contrast between communism and fascism is a good example of this fundamental distinction. Both systems are dictatorial, both crush any opposition, both have recourse to violence, and both are based on one-party systems. But these structural resemblances conceal a fundamental difference in orientation. Communism is revolutionary; it uses force to enable society to give birth to a new kind of social order. Fascism is conservative or reactionary; it uses force to prevent social change, to maintain the status quo, or to return to an even older social order.

☐ LEVEL OF ECONOMIC DEVELOPMENT To this distinction we must add still another, based on differences in the socio-economic level. Modern-day crises of social change or unforeseen contingencies occur at three different stages of development: sometimes they occur in countries enjoying a high level of economic growth—this was the case in 1929 in the United States, Germany, and Great Britain, and in France in 1956 when a structural crisis produced Poujadism; sometimes they occur in countries enjoying a moderate level of economic growth, in semi-industrialized nations—Russia in 1917 and the European popular democracies in 1945; and lastly, they may occur in countries with a low level of economic growth, in underdeveloped nations—crises in the newly independent States of Asia and Africa. Dictatorships and one-party systems take different forms, depending upon the level of development. The distinction between nazism (found in an advanced state of socio-economic development), and Italian or Spanish fascism (in a moderate state of development), and the feudal-type pseudo-fascism of underdeveloped countries, appears to be based on such socio-economic factors. The same distinction holds for Western communism and Chinese communism, the latter corresponding to conditions in underdeveloped countries. However, these distinctions remain rather vague in the absence of a careful sociological study of dictatorships.

□ ROLE OF THE PARTY WITHIN THE STATE   Finally, considerable differences exist between one-party systems depending on their role in the state and their importance. The party reaches its highest point in the communist parties, which form the very foundation of the state to such an extent that the party hierarchy has more power, practically speaking, than the state's official hierarchy. In fascist parties, the party role is generally less important, with many variations depending on circumstances. The Nazi party [National Socialist German Workers' party] performed certain essential functions, to which others were added during the Hitler regime. In Mussolini's Italy, the role of the Fascist party was much more modest; in certain respects, its importance actually seems to have decreased. More precisely, it passed through various stages of growth and decline. If it seemed advisable, Il Duce would shunt the party into the background to appease complaints from traditional quarters, or restore it to prominence if the latter forces appeared to be getting out of hand. In Spain, the Falange never played a leading role, and its influence continues to diminish. In Portugal, the National Union party exists more in theory than in practice.

The role of the one-party system varies not only according to its importance within the state, but also according to its character. A very significant difference is found here with respect to fascist and communist parties. The former serve primarily as the regime's Praetorian guard; as paramilitary organisms, their first task is to function as a police force and to maintain security. To be sure, they aim at organizing the nation and at spreading state directives, but since the organization is of a military rather than of a political nature, the propaganda is more simplistic and obsessive than educational. Communist parties, on the other hand, are first and foremost "the avant-garde of the revolution." They try to unite elements having the greatest enthusiasm and social awareness. Their main task consists of teaching and convincing others by means of a rational type of propaganda; also to spur activity in all domains of collective living; and finally, to act as the repository of doctrinal orthodoxy, which they interpret as the sovereign judges. Their role as a police force or as spies and informers is of secondary importance, and their role as a Praetorian guard is almost nonexistent.

Dominant Party Systems   I coined the expression "dominant party system" in 1951 to describe a broader phenomenon than the expression suggests in everyday usage. A party was termed "dominant" if it displayed the following two characteristics in a two- or a multiparty system: (1) it must clearly outdistance its rivals over an extended period of time (even if occasionally sustaining an electoral defeat); (2) it must identify with the nation as a whole—its doctrines, ideas, and even its style coinciding with those of the times. The Radical party, during a certain phase of the Third Republic, and social-democratic parties in Scandinavia, were the prototypes on which this definition of "dominant parties" was based. Today, the prevailing models of the "dominant party system" are provided by India and certain republics of Black Africa. We are dealing with an intermediate type of political system, midway between a pluralistic and a one-party system. The countries in question have several parties which vie with one another during elections—elections that are not plebiscites or referendums, but are truly competitive. Yet, among these parties, one is much larger than all the others. By itself it maintains an absolute majority of the parliamentary seats, with a wide margin to spare, and it seems to retain this comfortable majority over a long period of time. In governing, therefore, it is confronted with hardly any more obstacles than in a one-party system. Nevertheless, it must face up to criticism from the opposition, thereby maintaining a political dialogue. Hence, the spirit is quite different from that of a one-party system.

Granting all this, the notion of a "dominant party system" seems rather vague and imprecise in the last analysis. Among the countries in which the system is presently operating, we can discern roughly two types. On the one hand, India offers the example of a nation in which the opposition parties have a real existence; they garner a substantial number of votes and create a situation that is closer to a multiparty than to a one-party system. But certain African republics, on the other hand, are close to a one-party system since there is little more than token opposition to the dominant party, and the latter manifests fairly strong authoritarian tendencies. Indeed, in recent years these countries have moved, oftener than not, to a one-party system. The fact remains that the dominant party system corresponds in some degree to the social structure of underdeveloped societies on which Western powers have left their imprint; the very conditions for economic growth and modernization do not permit the functioning of a truly authentic pluralistic party system; the intellectual tendencies of their ruling elites are opposed to the one-party system. The dominant party system provides an intermediate solution. But this solution can work only if the balance of forces is such that domination is not threatened.

BIBLIOGRAPHY

On the general theory of political parties, the basic work is M. Duverger, *Les partis politiques*, 5th ed., 1964 (with bibliography);

for a sharp criticism of its methods, see G. Lavau, *Partis politiques et réalités sociales,* 1952. A summary of this appears in the article by M. Duverger, "Sociologie des partis politiques," in G. Gurvitch et al., *Traité de Sociologie,* Vol. II, 1961; we have borrowed extensively from it in our previous discussions. The student should also consult L. D. Epstein, *Political Parties in Western Democracies,* London, 1967; S. Neumann et al., *Modern Political Parties,* Chicago, 1956; A. Leiserson, *Parties and Politics,* New York, 1958; M. Manoïlesco, *Le parti unique,* 1936; M. Déat, *Le parti unique,* 1942; and the older but classical works of R. Michels, *Les partis politiques: essai sur les tendances oligarchiques des démocraties,* 1914 (translated from the German); M. Ostrogorski, *La démocratie et l'organisation des partis politiques,* 2 vols., 1903. Concerning political parties in the various European countries, see the bibliography at the end of the next chapter.

□ 2 □

EUROPEAN POLITICAL PARTIES

Modern political parties were first developed in Europe. The United States imitated the European technique, while introducing some rather significant changes. Subsequently, most countries throughout the world followed the same general course. Hence, European political struggles of the nineteenth century established, at least in part, the ideological frameworks within which the main political struggles of today unfold. The study of European political parties provides the best foundation for understanding all political parties. It is better to examine the subject closely in this relatively limited framework than to present a general picture of all the world's political parties—an effort that could only be extremely superficial.

The European political setting has the additional advantage of being sufficiently broad so that regional and local factors will not assume undue importance, as they would in a study confined to a single nation. It is also homogeneous enough if we examine only Western Europe—to give our comparisons validity, even if we carry them rather far. In the final analysis, the resemblances between the various European parties are greater than their differences. The political parties of England, Germany, France, Scandinavia, Italy, and so on rest on the same fundamental premises—a fact that is concealed when they are analyzed from a traditional national point of view, but which is made abundantly clear when they are studied from a comparative point of view.

THE HISTORICAL DEVELOPMENT OF EUROPEAN PARTIES

Modern political parties did not all originate at the same time. Some were born after World War II (for example, the French MRP, the Italian Christian Democratic party, the UNR). Others arrived on the scene between 1919 and 1939 (the communist parties and the fascist parties). Others appeared at the end of the nineteenth century or at the beginning of the twentieth, before 1914, including nearly all the socialist parties. Still others were formed in the first half of the nineteenth century, including most of the conservative and liberal parties. In all European countries, a picture of current political parties resembles that of a geological cross-section in which we see earth formations of different eras superimposed on one another: primary, secondary, tertiary, and quaternary.

The progressive development of European political parties revolved, first of all, around two basic conflicts: that between conservatives and liberals and that between socialists and capitalists. Today, the first of these has almost entirely disappeared, but the second one remains. By comparison, other conflicts are of secondary importance, although some of these have acquired considerable significance in certain countries where they have spawned new parties: communist, fascist, and Christian-Democratic, for example. Sometimes it is only a matter of a variation or modernization of one of the older basic conflicts.

THE TWO BASIC CONFLICTS

In the first half of the nineteenth century, European political life was dominated by the conflict between conservatives and liberals, a conflict dramatized by the French Revolution of 1789. After 1848, a second conflict appeared: the one between socialists and capitalists. At first, it interfered with the earlier struggle and finally replaced it. Both conflicts were simultaneously class struggles and ideological struggles, which eventually found expression in organized parties.

The Conflict between Conservatives and Liberals   The conflict between conservatives and liberals is now a thing of the past. Conservatives and liberals have often adopted the same or similar political views, and on occasion have even merged into a single party. But a century and a half ago, their confrontations often erupted into violence (the most vivid manifestation being the French Revolution of 1789 and the European revolutions of 1830 and 1848). The hostility between conservatives and liberals was so bitter in certain countries that some historians regarded them as evidence of the continuation of an unending struggle between the original inhabitants of a territory and the barbarian invaders of the first centuries of our era, but this theory is not taken seriously by anyone nowadays. The conflict between conservatives and liberals was not a struggle between two "races," as François Guizot and Augustin Thierry[1] believed, but rather a class struggle in which each class developed an ideology corresponding to its own interests.

[1] Guizot, minister of foreign affairs and prime minister under Louis Philippe, restored amicable relations with Europe and appealed to the thrift and prudence of France. An historian, Thierry enthusiastically embraced the ideas of the Revolution.

☐ THE BASIS: A CLASS STRUGGLE The conflict between conservatives and liberals was linked to a fundamental transformation of European society, in process since the Middle Ages.
In the ninth century, Europe was almost entirely dominated
by an agricultural economy, based on the exploitation of
feudal estates with a labor force comprised of serfs. It was
primarily a closed economy in which the large seignorial
domains were virtually self-sufficient, exchanges were very
limited, and life was essentially rural. Beginning in the tenth
century, there was a gradual revival of industry and commerce,
particularly in the cities. Alongside the aristocracy, the dominant social class in feudal society, there emerged a bourgeoisie,
the dominant class in commerical and industrial society. At
first the bourgeoisie was much weaker than the aristocracy,
which held in its hands the wealth of the land, military power,
and social prestige. But little by little, the development of
technical skills hastened the growth of industries and colonial
conquests, trade with Asia and the New World, and the expansion of the African slave trade spurred the development of
commerce and trade on a vast scale. The bourgeoisie became
increasingly richer, well educated, and highly competent, and
consequently found it more and more difficult to accept a
position of legal inferiority vis-à-vis the aristocracy.

The class struggle between bourgeoisie and aristocrats, as
early as the eleventh and twelfth centuries, contributed to the
movement of the Renaissance and the Reformation. It took
different forms in different countries. In Flanders, in certain
German cities, and in Switzerland, bourgeois principalities of
a sort were established within the framework of cities that
were more or less independent or allied with one another, like
the Hanseatic League. In Great Britain, the bourgeoisie se-
cured a regular representation with the king (House of Commons), concurrently with the aristocracy (House of Lords).
Moreover, many aristocrats were themselves involved in commerce or industry, which brought about an intermingling of
the two classes. In France, the bourgeoisie formed an alliance

of sorts with the monarchy in opposition to the *seigneurs,* leading eventually to a state of royal absolutism (Saint-Simon[2] clearly expressed the hostility of the aristocracy for a royalty that relied for support upon commoners rather than upon the aristocracy). At the same time, the bourgeoisie succeeded in gradually penetrating the ranks of the aristocracy through marriages or appointments to the *"noblesse de robe,"* conferred upon those who purchased certain public offices.

The progressive change in aristocratic agrarian societies remained inadequate, however, in relation to the evolving social and economic structures, especially since the latter were subjected to enormous scientific and technological advances in the eighteenth century. The aristocracy refused to surrender its hereditary privileges, which once corresponded to certain services performed in a feudal society—services very highly paid for by the common people—but which no longer had any basis. When the French nobles renounced their privileges (August 4, 1789) under the pressure of events, it was already too late. The bourgeoisie, conscious of playing an ever greater role in French society, became increasingly impatient about their inferior status. The Revolution of 1789 was the product of this fundamental struggle, aggravated by a number of special circumstances. By dramatizing the conflict, the Revolution heightened its intensity. It was to serve as a model—or as an incentive—for conflicts between liberals and conservatives throughout the nineteenth century.

In this conflict, then, liberals represented primarily the industrial, commercial, and intellectual bourgeoisie (those in the liberal professions), while conservatives represented the traditional aristocracy, based on the privileges of birth and land ownership. Writers, philosophers, and university people—the "intellectuals," as we call them nowadays—generally supported the bourgeoisie; they were to play a very important role in formulating liberal doctrines. The aristocracy, for its part, re-

[2] Duc de Saint-Simon (1675–1755), who wrote the famous *Mémoires* of the court of Louis XIV.

lied heavily upon the peasantry and rural population, which served, for the most part, as its "supporting class." This may seem strange at first glance, since peasants comprised the social class most clearly dominated and exploited by the aristocracy. But they were still largely illiterate, politically and socially uninformed, and they remained, on the whole, under the influence of a clergy that was generally very faithful to the aristocracy. The aristocracy used both the peasants' distrust of city dwellers and the support of the church to maintain its influence in the rural areas. Thus the liberal-conservative struggle took on the appearance of a conflict between town and country.

□ THE IDEOLOGICAL TRANSFORMATION OF THE CONFLICT Usually, it is the social class or group contesting the existing social order that first develops an ideology. One must present a picture, however sketchy, of the new order one wishes to substitute for the existing one if supporters are to be enlisted. The left is therefore more doctrinaire than the right. This law applies to the conflict between liberals and conservatives; the liberal ideology was developed first, and it was more complete and coherent than the conservative ideology.

It corresponded exactly to the primary interests of the class it represented. The bourgeoisie had no economic problems —at least not the middle and the upper middle classes (the *haute bourgeoisie*), who led the movement. They lived as well as the aristocracy, but the bourgeoisie were frustrated in their ambitions to expand because of one important obstacle: the legal inequality of status, determined by birth, which gave aristocrats a monopoly on certain military, governmental, political, and religious functions, as well as many other privileges. The notion that all men are born equal would therefore constitute the central theme of liberalism, a notion that has had far-reaching consequences. If all men are equal, then no one can command others unless he is empowered to do so by the

entire community. This principle led logically to the abolition of the monarchy and the establishment of an elective
power, based on national representation.

The notion of liberty was, in the final analysis, less important in liberal doctrine than the notion of equality. However,
bourgeois activities collided with government rules, regulations, and restrictions. Censorship and the absence of political
freedom impeded the development of liberal ideology; corporate interests, the protectionist trade policies of Colbert,[3]
and government economic policies put severe limitations on
commerce and industry. The *philosophes* and liberal intellectuals stressed the issue of liberty, which affected them most
directly. They made it the second pillar of liberal ideology,
along with equality. The bourgeoisie was far more concerned
with economic freedom, specifically, the abolition of corporations[4] and the prohibition of coalitions, trade unions, and
strikes. It agreed to accept compromises which would guarantee equality at the expense of a little less political freedom.
This was the basis of the First Empire [1804–14].

Even on the question of equality, liberals often dragged
their feet. The logical result of their doctrine of human equality would lead to the establishment of the republic and to
universal suffrage, but a limited, parliamentary monarchy with
a restricted number of voters seemed to them a less dangerous
course. For the bourgeoisie greatly distrusted the mass of the
population, in other words, the people. At the Constituent
Assembly of 1789, the bourgeoisie invented the ingenious
theory of "national sovereignty" to justify the possibility of
limited suffrage. Yet despite all this, liberal doctrine advanced
the idea of a republic and that of universal suffrage, which
alone were consistent with liberal principles. Broadly speaking,
although liberal ideology expressed, in the first instance, the
interests of the bourgeoisie, it went far beyond that. The

---

[3] Jean Baptiste Colbert, finance minister under Louis XIV.
[4] Actually craft unions with chartered privileges.

bourgeoisie helped the whole of mankind to enjoy greater equality and freedom because the liberal doctrine it formulated contained certain principles of universal value.

Conservative ideology is far less coherent and far less rational. To justify authoritarianism and inequality, its arguments are based primarily on "nature." Liberty and equality are perhaps desirable goals, but they are unattainable, they are utopian dreams. The truth is that men are unequal and cannot be otherwise. Moreover, it is preferable that this be so: reason thus corroborates nature. To achieve human progress, the best, the most intelligent, and the most capable should have authority over the others; only the domination of the elite over the masses guarantees the maintenance of civilization. For the development of the elite, education is of primary importance. The establishment of hereditary aristocracies, permitting the familial grouping of society's elites in an environment that is superior in culture, traditions, and refinement, will thereby provide the best means of perpetuating this elite class. Besides, authority is indispensable in the maintenance of any civilization to offset the constant pressure from the uncouth, uncivilized masses.

Rational justifications for conservatism were not necessary at the outset, for an ideology with little use for reason or the constructs of the mind; but gradually, a rationale was developed. Conservatives first found justification for social inequality, the aristocracy, the monarchy, and authoritarianism in their conformity to "nature" and to the divine will—synonymous expressions in a certain sense. When the struggle began between liberals and conservatives, there were no egalitarian republics except in a few small countries. All the great powers were monarchical and aristocratic. Hence, monarchy and aristocracy seemed to conform to the nature of things. An egalitarian republic seemed altogether fanciful. At the same time, religious beliefs were widespread and deeply rooted, and churches—particularly the Roman Catholic church—supported kings and aristocracies. In the twentieth century, when egalitarian republics multiplied and appeared "normal," and when religious influence declined and churches became less favorable to conservatism, it became necessary to develop rational justifications since arguments based on nature and religion had lost their effectiveness.

The Conflict between Socialists and Capitalists Between 1815 and 1848, the second industrial revolution occurred, producing an increase in both the size and number of factories. While the wealth and power of the bourgeoisie increased, and the latter continued to supplant the aristocracy, the working class itself multiplied in size. Its very concentration helped the spread of socialism, an ideology that crystallized working class aspirations and reinforced its struggle against the bourgeoisie.

□ THE BASIS: A CLASS STRUGGLE Like the preceding conflict, the one between socialists and capitalists was first of all a class struggle. The importance Marxism attaches to class struggles is understandable, for at the time when its doctrines were formulated, the primary political conflicts grew out of class conflict. The working class was born before the second industrial revolution and developed at the same time as the bourgeoisie, which used it. The employees and "journeymen" of the traditional trades and crafts formed the nucleus of the proletariat, to which were added workers in the manufacturing industries. But it was not yet very large, and above all, it was generally scattered and broken up into small business enterprises where relationships with the employer were more direct and informal. During the first half of the nineteenth century, on the other hand, large enterprises multiplied and became impersonal business corporations. There was a large population shift from the country to the cities, where an important part of the proletariat was concentrated—whose living conditions deteriorated drastically. No matter how hard a laborer worked (from fourteen to sixteen hours a day), he continued to be poor, while the business owners and managers grew wealthy. The struggle between the working class and the bourgeoisie, which had always existed (conflicts between journeymen and master craftsmen had been frequent), acquired a new magnitude and gravity that overshadowed all other conflicts.

We must note that this class struggle was very different from the one between the bourgeoisie and the aristocracy. The conflict between the bourgeoisie and the proletariat was a struggle between a dominated social class and the dominant class within the same system of production—industrial and commercial capitalism. The conflict between the bourgeoisie and the aristocracy was a struggle between two dominant social classes: the one, within the old feudal, agrarian production system that was in decline; the other, within the new capitalistic production system that was expanding. In the conflict between the bourgeoisie and the aristocracy, each of these two dominant classes succeeded in securing, to a substantial degree, the support of the class it dominated. We noted that the nobles were supported by the peasants. But the bourgeoisie also drew support from the workers, who were attracted at the outset by the liberal ideology, because of its principles of liberty and equality. The French Revolution of February 1848 was accomplished by the united efforts of the working class and the bourgeoisie, as were the revolutions of 1830 and 1789. But, here, we reach a turning point in the two conflicts. Shortly after the February Revolution, the conflict between the proletariat and the bourgeoisie was to override that of the conservatives and the liberals: the February alliance was shattered, and the bourgeoisie crushed the working class in a bloody struggle in June of 1848.

In its struggle, the proletariat found some support among the bourgeoisie, especially from the intellectuals. Socialist doctrines were formulated by theoreticians of bourgeois origins, including Marx, Engels, Lenin, and even Stalin, who became the first leaders of the socialist parties. While not numerically impressive, this support was nevertheless very effective. At a time when workers had very little schooling or education, they succeeded in finding enlightened leaders who were also educators, a fact that explains the highly doctrinaire nature of socialist parties. Their doctrine served not only to combat the opposition but also to educate, instruct, and enlighten the party membership. A second source of support for the working class came from a number of sons of the bourgeoisie, especially students, who took an active part in the political struggles of the nineteenth and twentieth century. Youth, which is more sensitive to injustice and naturally rebellious toward its elders, is inclined to adopt attitudes of this sort. During the conflict between liberals and conservatives, young noblemen made common cause with liberalism: for example, Lafayette and his friends in 1789. Support for socialism from young bourgeois students grew to much larger proportions.

□ THE IDEOLOGICAL TRANSPOSITION OF THE CONFLICT We cannot say here, as we did about the conservative-liberal struggle, that the class which attacks the existing social order is the first to develop its ideology, eliciting thereafter a response from the class in power. In this case, as a matter of fact, the economic doctrines of capitalism were formulated gradually, at the same time as the development of the bourgeoisie, and were directed first against medieval theories, and then against the doctrines of the physiocrats. They were revived to deal with socialism, after it appeared, but they existed before that. At the beginning of the nineteenth century, the economic theory of capitalism formed a coherent and complex system that was much more serious than socialistic doctrine, then still in its infancy. It was not until Marx that socialism acquired the same scope.

Also we must point out that the ideologies that developed in this instance were essentially economic in nature. Marx was to set up a complete philosophy, but one that placed its fundamental emphasis on economic structures. This was a true reflection of the nature of the struggle. The conflict between the bourgeoisie and the aristocracy had pivoted largely on questions of legal status. The bourgeoisie wanted to put an end to the hereditary privileges of the nobility, to royal power, and to infringements upon personal freedom by laws and regulations. But they did not make any demands of a purely economic nature, for, in this respect, they found themselves well off. On the contrary, the demands of the working class were primarily material and economic at the outset. The workers noted that, even if the laws established liberty and equality, these conditions did not in fact exist. Thus they were led to reflect upon the economic conditions needed for the exercise of freedom and equality.

The basic theme of socialist ideology is the exploitation of man by man within the framework of the capitalistic system. The Marxist theory of "plus-value" corresponds exactly to the conditions experienced by the proletariat in the nineteenth century. It matters little that Marx's analysis is debatable in certain details. The idea that the employer appropriates for himself a portion of the laborer's work, thereby "exploiting" and "alienating" the laborer, expressed what every worker could see with his own eyes as he worked fourteen to sixteen hours a day and remained impoverished, while his employer grew wealthy. For the working man, universal suffrage, an end to the privileges of the nobility, and a republican form of government were regarded as secondary goals; a far more urgent demand was to recover possession of the fruits of his labors in order to be able to live like a human being, and not like a proletarian crushed by poverty and exhausting, oppressive work.

The strength of socialist ideology was in its linking of material and political demands. It demonstrated that the ideals of liberty and equality, inscribed in constitutions and codes of law, remained mere "formalities," as long as the exploitation of man by man in the capitalistic system continued unchecked. On the one hand, the exploited and alienated proletarians did not have the means of actually exercising the freedoms granted them by law, and the legal equality they ostensibly enjoyed was simply ludicrous in the face of the enormous economic inequality they had to endure. On the other hand, the bourgeoisie, thanks to the material power it held through exploitation of the proletariat, controlled all the means necessary to nullify the exercise of liberty and equality by the masses. Accordingly, free elections were illusory since capitalists enjoyed a monopoly of the press and news media, thus insuring victory for bourgeois candidates. In addition, special interest groups manipulated elected officials and cabinet ministers, many of whom were dutifully obedient and compliant. Socialist criticism of "bourgeois parliamentarianism" was based on irrefutable facts. In the nineteenth century, it was a fairly accurate reflection of actual conditions; today, the development of labor unions and workers' parties has profoundly altered the situation.

The Overlapping of the Two Conflicts　From a long-range point of view, the conflict between liberals and conservatives was followed by the conflict between socialists and capitalists. Prior to 1848, there was only the liberal-conservative struggle, which today has all but disappeared while the socialist-capitalist struggle continues almost alone. But this substitution did not happen overnight. The two conflicts coexisted for a long time, and inevitably, they interfered with one another.

□　THE LIBERAL'S DILEMMA　The appearance of socialism put the liberals in a quandary: should they collaborate with the socialists against the conservatives, or should they, on the contrary, seek a reconciliation with the latter and make common cause with them against socialism? The second solution appeared the more logical since liberals were members of the bourgeoisie, the very class socialists regarded as their principal adversary. An alliance between the bourgeoisie and the proletariat seemed unnatural.

And yet it appeared possible in other respects. In the first place, the bourgeoisie and the working class had effectively fought together against the conservatives in the years preceding the development of modern industry and socialism. There were certain conflicts between the two classes during the Revolution of 1789, but these were secondary to their alliance against the aristocracy, which won for them their revolutionary victories. Moreover, these struggles together had developed among liberals of the left a relative understanding of economic and social problems. In 1794, the Jacobins displayed a certain broadmindedness in this area, and the "socialist-democrats" of 1848 were their heirs in this respect, as were the radicals of the first half of the twentieth century.

Furthermore, liberals and socialists were able "to travel a stretch of the same road together" (*"faire un bout de chemin ensemble"*), according to an expression which became famous during the Third French Republic. They were in complete disagreement as to ultimate goals, but they saw eye to eye on certain immediate reforms. For liberals, the principal objectives of political action were the abolition of inequities of birth, the establishment of universal suffrage, guarantees of political freedom, and the strengthening of the powers of Parliament. That was as far as they cared to go. Socialists wanted to go much farther, but they were also interested in the goals of the liberals. Of course, in the socialist view, liberty and equality could not be genuine as long as man continued to exploit his fellow man. But the establishment of a purely legal form of liberty and equality furnished some means in the struggle to put an end to man's exploitation of man. Universal suffrage, parliaments, and public freedoms permit the formation of workers' parties and labor unions, thanks to which socialism can develop more rapidly. An alliance between the bourgeoisie and the proletariat, against the monarchy and the aristocracy, was conceivable on this basis.

☐ THE ALTERNATIVES   In reality, the liberal parties' choice depended on the time and place. The foregoing analysis shows that the alliance between them and the socialists could only be a temporary one in any event. We can conceive of no more than a first phase of collaboration, followed inevitably by a rupture in the second phase. Still, the first phase could be a long one.

Generally, in countries where the conservatives still held power, and where political freedom and equality were non-existent at the time that socialism began to develop, the liberals tended to ally themselves with the socialists. Socialism was still too weak to be regarded as dangerous, and the alliance had a solid foundation, namely, the struggle against an aristocratic and monarchical social order and the establishment of political democracy. On the other hand, in countries where the conservatives had already become weak, where the liberal order was fairly well established, and where the aristocracy had lost its influence, the liberals tended to join forces with the conservatives and form a common front against the socialists. Conservatives accepted this alliance, first, because they, too, were interested in the defense of private property (which includes land holdings as well as factories and business enterprises); second, because the liberal social order seemed less objectionable to them, all things considered, than socialism. Moreover, with the passing of time, this liberal order came to look natural to the conservatives, and they gave it the veneration they traditionally show for the status quo.

Gradually, there was a tendency everywhere to move from the first situation to the second, to a split in the liberal-socialist alliance. However, neither this political change nor the initial choice was made without difficulties. A cleavage began to develop among the liberals, the right wing tending to join the conservatives and the left wing trying to collaborate with the socialists, or at least to maintain their independence. The transition from the first conflict (conservatives versus liberals) to the second conflict (socialists versus capitalists) thus tended to disrupt and fragment the liberal parties. Little by little, European liberal parties have dwindled in size and importance. In France, the break-up occurred in several stages, which we will examine further on. One group of liberals, the Radicals, have not yet merged with the conservatives. The current struggle within their ranks—between the supporters of the Democratic Center (with the MRP and the Independents) and those of a Social-Democratic Federation—indicates that certain elements are still opposed to this merger. In Great Britain, in the years between the two world wars, the Liberal party split in two, the National Liberals joining the Conservatives and the others remaining independent (but the influence of the independents has diminished greatly).

CONTEMPORARY CHANGE IN BASIC CONFLICTS

The two great fundamental conflicts of the nineteenth century have undergone profound changes in the twentieth century. The conservative-liberal conflict has virtually disappeared. However, certain traces of it remain, and it reappears in moments of crisis when the old conservatism reemerges in new forms like fascism. The socialist-capitalist struggle continues, but it is less bitter and intense because socialism is less revolutionary. There are those who think that socialism itself is in the process of disappearing. It is, moreover, often hidden and distorted by the communist problem.

The Evolution of Socialism The conflict between socialism and capitalism has evolved in two ways. It was first shaken by the Soviet Revolution of 1917, which produced a schism within the socialist parties. Subsequently, it was weakened as a result of the socialist movement toward reformism.

☐ THE COMMUNIST PROBLEM After the Revolution of 1917, the socialists were thrown into utter confusion. Certain groups refused to recognize the USSR as a true socialist regime; they felt, on the contrary, that the Soviet dictatorship had betrayed socialism, and they violently opposed the Soviets. This attitude appeared in the 1920's and was reinforced during the Stalinist era, especially at the time of the great trials in the 1930's and during the cold war from 1948 to 1953. Other groups believed that Russia, in spite of her faults and errors, had established the world's first socialist regime and that it was incumbent upon them to support it. Consequently, socialism was torn by a deep rift. In Germany and in France, the socialist parties split in two, half of them remaining faithful to pre-1917 socialism, the other half rallying to the support of Moscow and the new Internationale directed by the Russians (the Third Internationale). It was in this way the communist parties were formed, but their development was significant only in parts of Western Europe—in Germany from 1920 to 1933, in France and Italy since 1945. Elsewhere, the communists are very weak and have not caused any serious cleavage in socialist ranks.

The development of communist parties has obscured to some extent the conflict between socialism and capitalism. Socialist parties have often joined with "capitalist" parties in opposition to communism. To be sure, there have been periods of cooperation between socialists and communists, notably between 1934 and 1939, during the period of "Popular Fronts," and between 1941 and 1947, at the time of the Resistance movement and the war against Nazism. But these phases are much shorter than the periods of hostility between the two parties. The hostility was very pronounced between 1920 and 1934, and has become even more so since 1948 and the cold war. Consequently, the impression spread in the West that the real conflict was between the advocates of the Soviet system and the advocates of a pluralistic democracy in each country. This assessment is not an accurate reflection of the facts. Even at the height of the cold war, the majority of the communist voters in France and Italy did not accept the Soviet system and remained partial to a pluralistic democracy; opinion polls have clearly revealed this fact. Moreover, the advocates of pluralistic democracy—from socialists to conservatives—encompass a wide range of views.

Despite the tranquilizing influence of the international *détente,* the fear of communism remains an important factor in the internal politics of Western Europe, especially in those countries with powerful communist parties—France and Italy. But it is less a fundamental conflict than a means of camouflaging real social problems. The anti-communist reactions of the socialist parties drive them to form alliances with the center parties, and even with the right wing, rather than with the communists. If, in spite of everything, they do form a coalition with the communists, propaganda from the right and from the center raises the specter of "the Red peril," thereby causing the coalition to lose a number of "marginal voters" needed to win at the polls. Therefore, the left finds itself paralyzed in certain respects. However, this situation is changing. The formation of a governing alliance between communists, socialists, and agrarians in Finland, in May 1966, indicates how much things have changed since the 1950's. Likewise, an opinion poll taken in France, in February 1966, revealed that only 30 per cent of the citizenry were opposed to the inclusion of communist ministers in a government of the left.

☐ THE MOVEMENT TOWARD REFORMISM   From the beginning of socialism, two opposing tendencies developed within the party, one of them revolutionary, the other reformist. Partisans of the first approach maintain that it is not possible to demolish capitalism and build socialism except by a violent revolution, followed by a more or less prolonged period of dictatorship necessary to root out the last vestiges of bourgeois domination. Partisans of the second approach believe that the change from capitalism to socialism can be accomplished gradually through a series of strategic reforms. The reformist approach has always been stronger in English and Scandinavian socialism, and the revolutionary one in French and Italian socialism, while the two clashed in German and Austrian socialism. After 1917, communism embodied the revolutionary tendency and socialism, strictly speaking, embodied the reformist tendency. The French Socialist party (the SFIO) used the rhetoric of revolution until 1939, but long before that date, it had ceased being revolutionary to all intents and purposes. Nowadays, all European socialist parties are reformist. None of them dreams of overthrowing capitalism by revolutionary means, but only of changing the capitalistic system little by little, through the process of progressive reforms.

The communist parties in Western Europe have also begun to follow the same course. Most communist voters are no longer revolutionary, and have not been for some time now. A survey made in France in 1952 indicated this change, and a 1965 study furnished even stronger corroboration of the trend. In technologically advanced societies, even the most disadvantaged classes do not seek to overthrow the social order, for they fear that by destroying the very fragile and complex structure of modern industrial production, they would make their situation worse for a protracted period of time. Now, communist voters seek a gradual transformation of capitalist society far more than a violent revolution. Moreover, they have become attached to public freedoms and to a pluralistic democracy, as has the population generally. They no longer favor a one-party system and a dictatorship, even in the name of the proletariat. The example of Stalinism has clearly shown them the excesses one risks in adopting such a system. Even for the most oppressed class, political freedoms are no longer mere formalities, but something very real, and they do not want to lose them.

The leadership of the Western European communist parties lags behind this change in the average communist voter. But it will be difficult for the party leaders not to follow the rank-and-file, for the trend appears to be irreversible since it is closely tied to the development of modern industrial societies. In Italy, the leaders have been moving in this direction for the past several years. In France, they are slowly beginning to do the same thing. Moreover, a similar tendency is discernible in the Soviet Union and in the East European popular democracies, where the gradual "liberalization," under the pressure of technological development, is putting an end to monolithic structures and provoking a reexamination of the concept of the proletarian dictatorship. For the present, Western communist parties do not yet dare to call themselves reformists, for the term has always been in disfavor in communist circles. But they have started to become reform-minded and will doubtless continue in this direction. Henceforth, they will be able to use the term "revolutionary" only to describe the ultimate goal they wish to achieve, namely, a total change in social and political structures. But they cannot use the term to describe the means of attaining their objective, for they will inevitably become more and more reformist in their methods.

When they fully adopt this policy, their position will be almost the same as that of the socialists (with certain reservations we will discuss later). Consequently, the nature of the socialist-capitalist conflict is in a process of changing—the change having already occurred for the socialists, but still just developing among the communists. The struggle between socialism and capitalism has ceased to be a struggle *over* the regime and has become a struggle *within* the regime. There are already certain essential features of the Western system that socialists have no desire whatever to destroy, features that many communists also subscribe to in actual practice: the democratic structure, the pluralism of political parties, and freedoms the public enjoys. If they hope to eliminate certain other features of the existing regime—notably its economic structure—it will be done gradually, over a long period of time. Practically speaking, therefore, they will operate within the framework of the establishment for the foreseeable future.

☐ REFORMISM OR "CENTRISM"? Some think that socialist support for the establishment goes a great deal farther. Could it be that certain European socialists have abandoned the notion of effecting a complete change in economic structures, even as a long-range objective? German Social Democrats are only slightly socialistic; members of the English and Scandinavian labor parties are scarcely any more so; even the French Socialist party, the SFIO, is not much more militant than the others. When socialist governments are in power in Western Europe, they actually carry out very few reforms. Conservative and liberal governments, for their part, are compelled to make a few reforms in societies where the great majority of the voters are salaried employees, not capitalists.

Some believe, therefore, that there is no longer any real political conflict in Western Europe. On the political right, a few nostalgic liberals and conservatives dream of a possible return to complete capitalism; on the political left, a few "hard line" socialists entertain the visionary notion of establishing a socialistic society. The truth is that the industrial countries of Western Europe are mixed societies, with a large sector of the economy nationalized, with a more or less universal system of social security, and with a large degree of social planning. They cannot be otherwise. Conservatives and liberals work for the interests of owners and managers, while trying to limit somewhat the influence of the public sector and of social planning; socialists work for the interests of salaried employees, while trying to develop somewhat the public sector and to encourage social planning. Neither group can go very far, at least in the short term, and neither really wishes to. Thus, there is no longer any serious conflict between capitalism and socialism.

According to this view, political parties are moving toward a middle road, a position of "centrism." In Great Britain, Germany, and Scandinavia, political extremists have practically disappeared and centrism functions by alternating control of government between the center left (nominally socialist), or the center right (nominally conservative, liberal, or Christian Democratic), both groups differing only on details, not on matters of substance. In France and Italy, on the other hand, centrism is thought to be based on a quasi-permanent coalition between the moderates of the left (socialists) and the moderates of the right, while the extremists (communists and fascists) also counterbalance each other in a perpetual state of opposition. All of this results in a kind of political deadlock, together with a trend toward "depoliticization"; both phenomena can be explained in terms of a higher living standard that lessens social and political conflicts.

I have criticized these theories elsewhere; nothing warrants the assumption that Western industrial nations must remain immobilized in their present state of capitalism, tempered by social planning and some concern for the public sector. Certain other arguments lead one to believe just the opposite—that Western states are moving toward socialism. The present lack of political ardor among salaried workers, which is reflected in the moderation of the socialist parties, is due to the fact that, as of now, capitalist countries are wealthier and enjoy more freedom than the socialist countries. But this situation is not necessarily permanent either. For the moment, we can merely note the weakening of Western socialism and its rapprochement with the liberals and conservatives. However, important differences between the two types of parties remain. And we must not forget that in France and Italy, a large portion of the population votes with the Communist party simply to express its desire for a profound change in social structures: which is to say, an authentic kind of socialism, reformist in its methods, but revolutionary in its objectives.

This rapprochement between socialism and capitalism corresponds in some degree to changes in the social classes. The working class has become highly differentiated. Moreover, today it comprises only a minority of the vast army of salaried employees, whose ranks are also extremely diversified. And finally, differences in living standards and ways of life are not as great as they once were between capitalists and noncapitalists. European societies are moving, in certain respects, toward "middle class societies," which would provide a class basis for political centrism. However, we must not overestimate this trend, for there remains a fundamental difference between the salaried middle class and the capitalist middle class (businessmen, small industrialists, and members of the liberal professions). They do not have the same material interests or the same political attitudes. Nevertheless, it is true that social classes are more complex, more interwoven with one another, and more divided internally than they were a century ago, and the differences in their living standards today are less shocking. This explains why the conflict between the socialists and the capitalists has diminished. But if the class struggle has taken new forms, it has not disappeared; and it is doubtful whether socialists and capitalists could really merge in a centrist position.

The Change among Conservatives and Liberals The conservative-liberal conflict has almost completely disappeared. It reappears, however, under certain circumstances, when old-style conservatives try to use violence to defend the social order if they believe it to be seriously threatened. But except for such contingencies, conservatives and liberals tend to act in unison, although their historical differences occasionally make them reluctant to do so. Moreover, the recent growth of Christian Democratic parties has infused new life into conservatism and liberalism.

□ NEOCONSERVATISM AND FASCISM The conservative ideology of the nineteenth century no longer corresponds to the views and attitudes of Europeans in the twentieth century. Royalty and aristocracy may offer lucrative sources of revenue for illustrated magazines, but the public in general no longer believes in hereditary political power nor accepts the notion of hereditary privilege. Only a few small and uninfluential circles still maintain traditional conservative views. But conservatism has tried to give itself a new image, one that is better suited to the twentieth century. The development of socialism and communism frightens the middle classes. Their fear is all the greater because liberal regimes sometimes seem incapable of resisting pressure from the "Reds," if only because liberal principles oblige them to tolerate labor unions and socialist or communist political parties. A neoconservatism has exploited this fear by developing the idea that force alone can prevent the establishment of socialism or communism.

This new-style conservatism was born at the close of the last century under the influence of intellectuals like Barrès in France and Nietzsche in Germany. It first took the form of recourse to the military—"the call to the soldier" (*"l'appel au soldat"*)—which alone held the means of force capable of resisting the popular masses. On this rudimentary level, the idea took hold in Latin America and in many other parts of the world. The upheavals produced by the First World War, and then by the economic depression of 1929, gave it a great new impetus in Europe, as well as a new form—fascism. Fascism consists essentially in the invention of a new instrument of force, designed to compel obedience on the part of the masses: a party organized in the form of a militia which mobilizes an armed and disciplined elite, capable of controlling the entire population and of enforcing popular respect for its power. The political regimes of Mussolini's Italy and Hitler's Germany corresponded quite closely to this definition. In Portugal, Spain, and Eastern Europe, the conservative regimes established in the 1920's and 1930's were traditional military dictatorships rather than true fascist states.

Like communism, fascism was influential in only a part of Europe, unlike classic conservatism, liberalism, and socialism, which developed everywhere. To be sure, in the years from 1934 to 1939, fascist parties were to be found almost everywhere—even in Great Britain, the Netherlands, and Scandinavia. But they were of real importance only in Italy and Germany, where they came to power, and in France, with the Leagues, the French Social party and the French Popular party (in Belgium, rexism, allied with Flemish nationalism, also had a significant following). The Second World War, the defeat of Mussolini and Hitler, and the revelation of the horrors committed by the Nazis dealt a very serious blow to fascism after 1945. However, it has not entirely disappeared. In Italy, the Italian Social Movement, which is neofascist, won more than a million and a half votes and twenty-seven seats in Parliament. In Austria, neo-Nazism seems to have a certain influence. In France, during the period from 1958 to 1962, the repercussions from decolonization, and particularly from the war in Algeria, generated sympathy for authoritarian movements of the extreme right, which had been very weak up to that time. If fascism is an offshoot of conservatism, from an ideological point of view it found support among a large number of the bourgeoisie, even though the latter/had been liberal in the nineteenth century and remains so under normal conditions. We have already pointed out that the bourgeoisie, in its struggle against the aristocracy, preferred equality to freedom, but in its demands for liberties the bourgeoisie was more insistent on economic than on political freedom. In its struggle against the proletariat and against socialism, the same phenomena appeared. Although the European bourgeoisie is very fond of political freedom, it is even more devoted to private property. Fascism shows that it will sacrifice the former for the latter. The same is true of the wealthy, capitalistic bourgeoisie, which aided Hitler and Mussolini, and of the *petite bourgeoisie,* which is in constant fear of being reduced to the state of the proletariat and, for this reason, despises socialism. Fascism develops from a coalition of these two elements. However, in the south of Italy, in Spain, and in Portugal—less industrialized societies—we see, instead, the traditional conservative coalition of large landowners and peasants as the mainstay of the regime. The result, therefore, is not genuine fascism.

It is conceded nowadays that the danger of fascism is not great in Western democracies, in normal times. The population as a whole strongly desires political freedom, freedom from the terrors of a police state, political pluralism, and the possibility of expressing opposition to government policies. We might say that these conditions make for a generally comfortable situation. In a highly developed industrial society in which the standard of living is high and the security of the great majority is virtually assured, fascism and neoconservatism do not normally find favorable ground for development. However, this optimism is predicated only on the absence of any serious economic crisis such as the one that triggered a tidal wave of fascist movements in the 1930's. If the foundations of prosperity begin to crumble in a highly developed society, where the population is attached to its material comforts and its high standard of living, then there is reason to fear that the mass of the people, disoriented and in distress, might turn in any direction. It is true that economists are convinced the means now exist to prevent a serious crisis of the kind that occured in 1929. But other upheavals can produce disorientation that is conducive to fascism: the development of McCarthyism in the United States during 1952–53, following the victory of communism in China, is clear evidence of such a possibility.

☐ THE TENDENCY TOWARD FUSION Whatever else may be said of them, neoconservatism and fascism appear to be exceptional political phenomena, occurring only in periods of crisis. The normal development of European conservatism in the twentieth century leans in another direction—toward a fusion with liberalism. Little by little, monarchical and aristocratic regimes have disappeared or have become mere formalities, like the House of Lords and the British Crown, and the Scandinavian royalty. The liberal order has spread everywhere and gained acceptance by nearly everyone. A few English lords, a few country squires in rural France, a few Bavarian or Austrian aristocrats, and a handful of Italian princes preserve a nostalgia for "the good old days"; but they have no more illusions about their possible return than the likelihood or reviving sedan chairs, harpsichords, and crinoline hoopskirts. The liberal regime having become "the established order," conservatives are therefore quite naturally inclined to support it. Moreover, the liberal order is not unfavorable to them. Since the time of Louis-Philippe in France [1830–48], and for a much longer time in Great Britain, the nobility has engaged in business and done very well at it. The defense of private property, free enterprise, and capitalism against socialism and communism is henceforth as important to them as to the bourgeoisie. Consequently, the liberal and conservative parties, fierce enemies in the nineteenth century, tend to merge with one another in the twentieth century.

In Great Britain, the coalition is still only partial. The Liberal party split into two groups, the National Liberals joining the Conservative party, while others maintained an independent Liberal party; but supporters of the latter gradually deserted it. We should note that the British Conservative party actually defends nineteenth-century liberalism: its name is Conservative, its program is liberal. In France, the liberals formed two groups at the beginning of the Third Republic [1870]—the "progressives" or "opportunists" and the radicals. The first group split in two in 1900, its right wing joining a large number of conservatives in the Republican Federation, and its left wing remaining independent under the name of the Democratic Alliance. Between 1919 and 1939, the Republican Federation included almost all of the old conservatives together with the moderate liberals. After 1945, the Republican Federation and the Democratic Alliance merged within the body of the "Independents." Only the radicals resisted this integration with the moderate right; after hesitating for a long time between the right and the left, they entered the Federation of the Democratic and Socialist Left in 1965.

The situation among the remaining liberal parties in Western Europe is rather paradoxical. In general, they have become small parties, unable to govern alone and capable only of providing marginal support for one group or another. This often leads them to take demagogic stands. Freer in their movements than the large political parties, they sometimes tend to abuse their freedom. They are not above appealing to middle classes and *petite bourgeois* malcontents on more or less Poujadist[5] themes—resistance to taxation and even ultra-nationalism. Thus, on the one hand, these parties remain faithful to the liberal tradition of the nineteenth century, but, on the other hand, some of them turn their backs on that tradition by favoring revolutionary movements close to those of the far right. In this connection, the situation of the German Liberal party is characteristic. We can compare it with the Austrian Liberal party, which is still closer to a kind of neo-Nazism. Even in France, during the Algerian war, certain radical groups favored the ultranationalists.

In any event, the fusion of conservatives and liberals did not occur without any difficulty. Historical traditions and party structures both posed problems; indeed, the "persistence of structures" was very strong here. Also one ideological barrier, which still arises on occasion, impeded the union of conservatives and liberals into a single party—religion. It has been said that European conservatives in general have relied upon religion, especially the Catholic religion, to attain their political objectives. In certain countries, such as France, Austria, Belgium, and Italy, this has caused political battles to digress into the religious domain. In particular, the question of schools—public schools or religious schools—has assumed great importance. These controversies, which have persisted to the present day, explain the different feelings of a Radical and a man of the right or a Popular Republican in France; the difference between a Liberal and a Social Christian in Belgium and Italy. They maintain a division between political parties whose positions are almost identical on all other issues. The development of Christian Democratic parties has not yet fully resolved the problem.

[5] Pierre Poujade led a right-wing party, the Union for the Defense of Tradesmen and Artisans, that opposed taxation and played a significant role in the defeat of Pierre Mendes-France in the 1956 elections.

□ CHRISTIAN DEMOCRATS   The Christian Democratic parties are hard to classify. In 1945, the French MRP collaborated with the communists and the socialists in a "tripartite" government, which enacted social security and nationalized a number of industries. At that time, the MRP reflected undeniable socialistic tendencies. Twenty years later, it opposed and defeated the Social Democratic Federation proposed by Gaston Deferre (June 18, 1965) because the latter was too socialistic, and its president decried the notion of "collectivism." In the 1965 national presidential elections, the MRP tried to rally all the non-Gaullist right around the candidacy of Jean Lecanuet. Lecanuet has since sought to unite the MRP, Independents, and Radicals of the right into a "Democratic Center," which would be a conservative party. In Italy, the powerful Christian Democratic party unites under its banner traditional conservatives, Christian liberals, plus, oddly enough, a number of socialistic groups. In the West German Federal Republic, the CDU–CSU [Christian Democratic Union–Christian Socialist Union] includes only conservative and liberal elements; there are no groups on the left close to the socialists. Likewise, the Dutch and Belgian Social Christians are unequivocally situated in the "capitalist" camp. In the final analysis, Christian Democracy is a modern version of conservative and liberal tendencies, although it had hoped to move more to the left and establish a bridge with socialism.

In the nineteenth century, some Christians broke away from the conservatives and were leaning toward liberal ideas (very advanced at that time) as well as a certain type of socialism. Robert de Lamennais, and other democratic priests of the nineteenth century, Marc Sangnier, and *Le Sillon,* prior to 1914, embodied this tendency in France. In Germany, persecution by Bismarck—the *Kulturkampf* [6]—gave birth to the Catholic Center party, the first Christian Democratic party. By calling itself "center," the party affirmed its determination to

[6] The conflict between the Roman Catholic church and the German government under Bismarck.

represent a Catholicism independent of the conservative right. And, indeed, it sometimes joined forces with socialists even before 1914. Between 1920 and 1933, the Catholic Center party collaborated regularly with the Social Democrats to form the Weimar coalition, resisting both the communists and right-wing extremists, but eventually, it voted for the law granting full powers to Adolf Hitler. In Italy, the "Popular party," founded by Don Sturzo in 1920, also sought to maintain a centrist position; however, it collaborated with Mussolini at the beginning of his political career.

The proliferation of Christian Democratic parties in Western Europe occurred at the time of the Liberation in 1944–45. In their resistance to Nazism, Christian groups worked with the socialists and the communists, forming the cadres of the large Christian Democratic parties that were founded at that time and enjoyed great success at the polls—the French MRP, the Italian Christian Democrats, and the German Christian Democratic Union. In Italy and France, they took part in governments of the left, but their principal activity was in curbing revolutionary movements and in preventing communist domination. Accordingly, they served as a haven for many conservative voters who, in the last analysis, preferred these "Christian Reds," whom they disliked, to the "out-and-out" Reds, whom they feared even more. In France, these voters later filtered back into right-wing parties; in Italy, they remained much more faithful to Christian Democracy; and in Germany, the Christian Democrats gradually attracted all the voters of the right and the center right, except for those who remained loyal to the small liberal party.

Finally, there are two types of European Christian Democratic parties. Some, like the Dutch and Belgian Social Christian parties and the Austrian Popular party, are purely and simply conservative parties that have changed their name—a phenomenon associated with the similar resurgence of most conservative parties. The German Christian Democrats are close to this category, although they are in a special situation:

they represent the merger of several earlier conservative and moderate tendencies. Other Christian Democratic parties, such as the French MRP and the Italian Christian Democratic party, are situated in the center of the political spectrum, distinct from the conservative parties that remain on their right. Parties in this category are willing to try to form centrist combinations with the socialists—even some of the conservative Christian Democrats occasionally try this too.

The difference between the two types is not very great. All Christian Democratic parties remain close to the center right, where the old liberal and conservative parties also converge. It is sometimes suggested that they encourage this convergence as a means of seeing religious problems in a new light and especially, for putting an end to clericalism. Actually, they have not been very successful in this respect. In Austria, Italy, Belgium, and the Netherlands, the parties have remained strongly clerical. The German CDU is a little less so because it aims to be interdenominational. The French MRP, which had made several attempts in this direction, has fallen back into the old rut regarding private and parochial schools. Changes in the church itself, since Vatican II, are much more audacious, at least in theory. The principal contribution of the Christian Democratic parties is to have given the center right a new appeal and a more open-minded approach to the problems of the twentieth century. As such, they reflect the new style of capitalism that today characterizes Western Europe. This also accounts for their overtures to centrist socialism. They express, on the political right, the hope for an industrial society based on a broad middle class, in which the class struggle will disappear—a hope that is also found on the left among moderate socialists.

THE INTERFERENCE OF NATIONAL PROBLEMS

The conflicts we have just examined—conflicts between conservatives and liberals, between socialists and capitalists, and their evolution in the twentieth century—are common to all European countries, or at least most of them. In each country, these general conflicts have combined with particular local factors, which fall into two categories. Some give rise to parties based on new ideologies or new social classes, different from those we have just described. Others simply produce cleavages within the fundamental tendencies.

Divisions within Fundamental Tendencies   Let us take, for example, the Social Christian party, the "Anti-Revolutionary" party, and the "Historical Christian" party of the Netherlands. They are not separated by any basic differences in their social class or in their political ideology; all three are conservative parties. This subdivision of a common political tendency into three parties was the result of religious factors. In France, institutional and historical factors have been responsible for similar divisions.

☐   SCHISMS CAUSED BY RELIGIOUS FACTORS   As we have already indicated, religion has generally been used in Europe by political parties of the right. Conservatives used religion in their struggle against the liberals. Capitalism has done the same thing in its struggle against socialism and communism. There are a few exceptions to this general rule: Belgian Catholics formed an alliance with the liberals during the anti-Dutch Revolution of 1830 (directed against a country with a Protestant majority), but thereafter, they resumed their opposition to the liberals; and German Catholics formed a center party at the end of the nineteenth century. Protestants have generally been less conservative than Catholics—in France, they supported liberalism rather than conservatism. In any event, religion was a help to one party or the other, but it did not cause the appearance of new parties. It supported one ideological tendency or another, but it did not create a rift in any single party.

In certain countries with religious pluralism, conflicts between churches have been superimposed on strictly political conflicts, leading to the appearance of several tendencies within the same political family. The case of the Netherlands, which we have already mentioned, deserves closer scrutiny. In the nineteenth century, both Catholics and Protestants were conservatives. But their religious antagonisms and their traditional rivalry were too strong to permit them to collaborate within the framework of a single party. Therefore, they formed two conservative parties, one of them Catholic, the other Protestant. The Catholic conservatives collaborated with the liberals for a long time in order to weaken the Protestants. Later, Catholic and Protestant conservatives drew closer together, but there were those among the Protestants who would not accept this collaboration with the "Papists." A rift then developed within the Protestant conservative party, splitting it into "antirevolutionaries" and "historical Christians." For religious reasons, then, Dutch conservatism was divided into three parties.

☐ SCHISMS PRODUCED BY HISTORICAL OR INSTITUTIONAL FACTORS The most typical example is that of France. At the beginning of the nineteenth century, conservatives and liberals subdivided into at least two groups, the extremists and the moderates. Among the conservatives, there were the *ultras,* who called themselves *légitimistes* after 1830, and the more moderate monarchists known as *Orléanistes* under Louis Philippe [1830–48]. Among the liberals were the militant, doctrinaire Jacobins and the regular, more moderately inclined, liberals. This double rift is explained by the violence of the Revolution of 1789 and the reaction that ensued. Compelled by events to establish a regime far too advanced for the society of their time, the Jacobins had to resort to terroristic tactics (the Reign of Terror) in order to maintain the regime; moderate liberals rejected these methods and subsequently refused to collaborate with those who had used them. To take revenge on the Red Terror, certain conservatives, in their turn, created the White Terror, which likewise alienated the moderates in their camp. On the one hand, the traditions of 1793 drove many socialists to commit acts of violence. Revolutions in the style of Blanqui[7] were more numerous in France than anywhere else; they caused the more reform-minded socialists to form a separate organization. On the other hand, the traditions of 1815 drove the political right to repress socialism more harshly than elsewhere. The repression carried out in June 1848 and especially the repression of the Commune of Paris [1871] are without parallel in Western Europe. This naturally hardened socialist positions and strengthened their revolutionary tendency.

A second source of ideological dissension arose in France, concurrently with the first: the attitude to take toward the swift succession of regimes. Until 1871, no political regime lasted more than fifteen to eighteen years, and many were even more short-lived. The problem of deciding whether to act within the framework of the existing regime, or to attempt first to establish another regime, thus assumed very great importance. Accordingly, the conservatives wondered whether they should collaborate with the Constituent Assembly of 1789, with Napoleon I, with Louis Philippe, with the Second Republic, with Napoleon III, and with the Third Republic— or whether they should seek to overthrow them. Liberals asked the same question about those regimes, and also about the Restoration. Socialists faced the same dilemma under the Second Republic, under Napoleon III, and under the Third Republic. The same problem reappeared in our own day with the Vichy government and the present Fifth Republic. Among the conservatives, we find not only the *légitimistes* and the *Orléanistes*, but also *Bonapartistes* and *Républicains;* among the liberals, not only Jacobins and moderates, but also splinter groups of *Bonapartistes, Orléanistes,* and *Républicains* during the Second Empire [1852–70]. Clearly, the *Orléanistes* and the *Bonapartistes* are heterogeneous parties, composed of diverse elements. Between 1940 and 1944, all parties had their resist-

[7] Louis Auguste Blanqui (1805–81), a socialist and life-long revolutionary.

ance groups, their Vichy supporters, and their Nazi collabora-
tors. Since 1958, all parties have their Gaullists and their anti-
Gaullists. The dual phenomenon of the cleavage among extremists and moderates on the one hand, and the divisiveness
produced by frequent changes in political regimes on the other,
accounts for the greater multiplicity of parties in France, and
above all, their weak internal organization and their indistinct
lines of demarcation.

New Tendencies In other European states, national factors
have produced political parties founded on new social classes
or new ideologies, unlike those we have been examining. The
two main types consist of parties formed by peasants and rural
groups, and parties of a nationalistic nature. The former are
based on a social class; the latter, on a socio-cultural complex,
in the sense that we have previously given this term.

□ PEASANT PARTIES In most Western European countries,
the peasantry has not been organized into distinct parties.
Rather, as we have pointed out, it generally served as a supporting class, first for the aristocracy against the bourgeoisie,
then for the bourgeoisie against the proletariat. It therefore
tended to support conservative parties in the nineteenth century, and thereafter anti-socialist parties. Of course, the situation is not quite so simple, or the peasantry quite so homogeneous. In France, radicalism had substantial support from the
peasants during the Third Republic, as did socialism thereafter. Certain rural areas voted communist long before 1939.
Moreover, a few independent peasant parties have tried to
become organized, but with little success.

In Scandinavia, however, the peasantry organized into a
party that was distinct from both conservatives and liberals,
but its position with respect to each of these groups was not
always clear. In Sweden, for example, the Lantmanna party,
founded in 1867, wavered between conservatism and liberalism
before it gave birth to the present-day Conservative party. But

another peasant party then reappeared in 1913. In Norway, the peasant movement was first allied with the Liberal party before breaking away and moving to the right. In Denmark, the Peasant party first formed an alliance with the conservatives, but then turned toward liberalism and became one of the founders of the modern *Venstre* (left). In Finland, the Agrarian party has always had a liberal tendency, even radical, because it relied primarily on the very small farm operators.

Why have peasant parties developed in Scandinavia, but not in the rest of Western Europe? The question has never been thoroughly studied. It must be noted, first of all, that the northern countries were never part of feudal society with its traditional tie binding the peasant to the seignorial domain. Denmark was the only Nordic state ever to prohibit peasants from leaving the property on which they were born, and this situation lasted for only a relatively short period of time— from 1733 to 1784. Accordingly, in Scandinavia, the free peasants were a more important group than their counterparts elsewhere. They were not controlled or regimented by noblemen, whom they would have come to regard as their natural representatives. Moreover, the free peasants were actually represented in the royal parliaments. Whereas in France, the Estates General was made up of three "orders"—clergy, nobility, and Third Estate (the last drawn from the urban bourgeoisie)— and in England, Parliament was comprised of the ecclesiastical and secular lords, and the Commons representing the bourgeoisie, the Swedish Parliament of 1634 included four "estates" —clergy, nobility, bourgeoisie, and peasantry. Consequently, an independent peasant class was accustomed to having an organized, independent representation in the government.

☐ NATIONALIST PARTIES In our use of the term "nationalist parties," we are referring to parties that demand the independence of a nation which is under the domination of another. These parties represent a social group rather than a class—a horizontal group, cutting across class lines, a national group incorporated into a state where it feels alien and desires to be a state in its own right. This situation was very common in nineteenth-century Europe, when nationalist movements were extremely numerous and militant, in states like Germany, Austria, Italy, and Spain. In the twentieth century, we find the same situation in the Balkan states, in Belgium, and especially in colonial states. All the dependent national groups did not form separate and independent parties. Many of them, in the last century, supported the liberal parties which, for that reason, were known in certain countries as "national liberal parties." Today, communist parties express certain demands for national independence.

But more often, a national group's demands for independence or autonomy are expressed by a new political party which is thus added to those already produced by other political conflicts: Polish parties, Czech parties, Croatian parties before 1914, the Irish party in Great Britain before Ireland's independence, the Sudete German and Slovak parties in Czechoslovakia before 1939, the Flemish nationalist parties in Belgium, the Basque and Catalan parties in the Spanish Republic, and so forth. It would be particularly interesting to study the case of the African nationalist parties during the Fourth French Republic. Instead of following a policy of ruthless opposition to other French parties, they generally formed alliances with them in order to obtain reforms in Africa; this was the strategy the Irish nationalists used at the beginning of the century in the British Parliament, where they supported the Liberal government.

We must not confuse the nationalist parties, as we have defined them, with the use of nationalism as a rallying cry for conservative and fascist parties since the end of the nineteenth century. The latter groups are not concerned with demands for national independence or with defending a people's right to self-determination; they are concerned, instead, with vaunting a nation's pride, with asserting its superiority over other nations, and with nurturing its hatred of its enemies. This furnishes justification for imposing authoritarian and unpopular measures within the country, for artificially developing a national solidarity, and for camouflaging the domination of one social class over another behind an image of national unity directed against "the common foe." This kind of nationalism constitutes a smokescreen rather than an ideology in any legitimate sense of the term.

AN OUTLINE OF PRESENT-DAY EUROPEAN PARTIES

It seems that we can now classify all European political parties into two main categories. First, there are those whose primary objective is to maintain the economic and social structures of liberal capitalism; their first reaction is always favorable to private enterprise and unfavorable to government intervention or to collective solutions, even if they finally concede that the state is sometimes obliged to intervene and that certain problems can only be resolved through community action. These include the conservative, liberal, and Christian Democratic parties, except for a few small groups among the Christian Democrats. Second, there are those whose primary concern is with the public interest, without first considering the protection of private corporations and business interests; they are naturally inclined to favor government intervention and collective solutions. This category includes the socialist and communist parties and a few elements among the radical left and the Christian Democrats. We cannot give a more precise definition of Western socialism since many European socialists accept in fact a general continuation of the capitalist society, which they simply seek to modify or rearrange. Only the communists and left-wing socialists desire a total overthrow of Western economic and social structures. Or at least, that is what they say.

We will not examine European parties according to this

classification of right and left. While it would have the advantage of permitting a comparison between parties in the same political family from one country to another, we have already made such a comparison in the preceding historical analysis. Studying contemporary European parties in an ideological framework would prevent our highlighting the diversity of the party systems in Europe. Now this diversity is a matter of great importance, for it explains the different ways that parliamentary regimes function in the various European countries. Therefore, we will take as our frame of reference for a comparative analysis, not the political parties themselves or the party families (right and left), but the European party system. From this standpoint, there are two main types: the dualistic or para-dualistic systems and the multiparty systems.

THE DUALISTIC OR PARA-DUALISTIC SYSTEMS

No European country has a two-party system in the strict sense of the word. In Great Britain, for example, a third party, the Liberals, obtained 5.9 per cent of the votes in the 1959 elections and six seats in Parliament; in the 1964 elections, the same party received 11.2 per cent of the votes and nine parliamentary seats. In addition, there is a Communist party and a handful of small fascist groups. But from a practical standpoint, we can describe a system as dualistic when two large parties are so powerful that normally, one or the other has an absolute majority of the seats in Parliament, enabling it to govern alone without forming an alliance. In such a situation, the small parties are virtually outside the political arena. This has been the case in Great Britain since 1935. To be sure, the revival of the Liberal party in recent years means that one day soon it could possibly gain enough deputies to keep either the Conservatives or the Labourites from governing by themselves. But, it seems that such a situation would be exceptional and only temporary.

We designate as "para-dualistic" systems in which two large parties dominate political life, but neither of which is normally able to obtain a parliamentary majority by itself. Consequently, they must either form a coalition with a third party or between themselves. These para-dualistic systems should not be confused with a "pseudo" or flexible two-party system, of which the United States provides an excellent example: a two-party system without strong internal discipline, in which the majority held by one party or the other has little meaning since its members almost never vote "a straight party line." Para-dualism proper is characteristic of West Germany, Belgium, and Austria.

The British Two-Party System   Great Britain is the model for the two-party system, just as it was the model for the parliamentary regime. Moreover, the two phenomena are not unrelated: it is because of the two-party system that the parliamentary regime functions so well in Britain, while its absence on the continent makes parliamentary government difficult.[8] However, the British two-party system has experienced crises, and the renaissance of the Liberal party could create new ones.

□   FROM ONE TWO-PARTY SYSTEM TO ANOTHER   Britain's two-party system rests on a long tradition. As early as 1641, Gardiner noted that "two parties oppose each other in the House of Commons," but these were, properly speaking, factions rather than parties. A few years later, they were to be known as "Tories" and "Whigs," nicknames given in a spirit of derision (the Tories were bandits on the highways of Ireland, the Whigs a band of Scottish insurgents in 1648). In the middle of the nineteenth century, Whigs and Tories adopted the modern names of Liberals and Conservatives, gradually organized into genuine political parties, and soon established solid electoral machines at the party base and well-disciplined parliamentary

[8] On this question, see Maurice Duverger, *Institutions politiques et droit constitutionnel,* 8th ed., pp. 273ff.

groups at the party summit. In no other European country was the conflict between conservatives and liberals conducted with such highly developed political instruments. The Liberal party under Gladstone was in power from 1868 to 1874, then again from 1880 to 1886; the Conservative party under Disraeli was in power from 1874 to 1880, then again from 1886 to 1906.

In 1900, the Congress of Trade Unions created a socialist party organization which, in 1906, took the name of "Labour party." Until 1922, however, this third party did not prevent the Conservatives or Liberals from gaining a parliamentary majority. It was not until 1922 that the Labourites surpassed the Liberals, becoming the country's second largest political party with 142 seats in Parliament. From then on, the Liberal party lost ground, and Great Britain experienced a three-party political system whose unstable ruling coalitions resembled those of French governments. By 1935, the Liberals were so weak that one of the other parties—Conservative or Labourite —could command a majority by itself. Hence dualism was reestablished. Great Britain thus passed from a nineteenth-century two-party system to a twentieth-century two-party system, with the second replacing the first through the elimination of the third party.

☐ THE CHANGES IN THE SYSTEM The British two-party system went through two crises when a third party prevented either of the two larger parties from winning an absolute majority. The first, lasting from 1910 to 1918, was caused by a powerful Irish nationalist party, which held eighty seats in the House of Commons. The second crisis, from 1922 to 1935, corresponds to the development of the Labour party and the decline of the Liberal party, which is to say, the transition period between the two-party system of the nineteenth century and that of the twentieth.

Although the Irish nationalists had held more than eighty seats in Commons before the 1910 elections, that fact had not prevented either of the two major parties from securing a parliamentary majority (402 Conservative seats out of a total of 670 in 1900; 411 Liberal seats in 1906). In the elections of January 1910, however, the Liberals won 275 seats and the Conservatives 273. After the dissolution of Parliament, elections held in December 1910 gave 270 seats to the Liberals and 273 to the Conservatives. Government by a single party was no longer possible. This was not just because of the Irish nationalists, but also of the Labourites, who made inroads among the Liberals (they won 29 seats in 1906, 40 in January 1910, and 42 in December 1910). Until the First World War, the Liberals formed an alliance with the Irish nationalists, to whom they granted "Home Rule." During the war, all parties suspended hostilities in the interest of national unity. In 1918, the Conservatives succeeded in securing a majority of their own in Parliament.

The crisis in Britain's two-party system between 1910 and 1918 was due less to the Irish nationalists than to the growth of the Labour party, which captured votes and seats from the Liberals. Even without the Irish deputies, neither of the two major parties could have held a parliamentary majority from 1910 to 1918. In 1906, the appearance of a Labour party, representing the working class and a socialist ideology, began to undermine the Conservative-Liberal two-party system. It was thirty years before the Labourite-Conservative two-party system replaced it. The period from 1922 until 1935, when the Liberals were virtually eliminated from the political scene, was characterized by a three-party system. Despite this three-way contest, the Conservatives won an absolute majority of the parliamentary seats in 1922 (344 out of 615), in 1924 (419 seats), and in 1931 (473 seats). But this majority of seats corresponded to a minority of the votes cast in 1922 (5,500,000 out of 14,400,000) and in 1924 (7,450,000 out of 16,650,000)— a factor that made it difficult to govern effectively. In the elections of 1923 and 1924, no single party obtained a majority, and it was necessary to form alliances. The result was governmental, and even parliamentary, instability (the 1923 legislature lasted one year; the 1929 legislature lasted two years).

Some observers are wondering whether the revival of the Liberal party since 1959 might not lead Britain into a new crisis. The Liberals, who had received only 700,000 votes in the 1951 elections, picked up 1,600,000 in 1959, and nearly 3,100,000 in 1964 (11.9 per cent of the votes cast). They have also reorganized their party, which has recently gained new members. Since the margin between Labourites and Conservatives is narrow, it is possible that one day neither of them would be able to muster a majority, putting the Liberal party in a decisive position. This could mark a return to the unstable situation of 1922 to 1935, but such an eventuality is unlikely. Dissolving the Parliament and obliging the electorate to make a clear choice in the matter would very likely suffice to return a majority to one of the two major parties. The difference between 1922–35 and the present situation is that the Liberal party remains much weaker than either of the other two. Labourites and Conservatives each received four times as many votes as the Liberals in 1964, and eight times as many in 1959. Nor can we detect any solid base on which the Liberals might develop and become again the country's second party.

Para-Dualistic Systems No other European country has a two-party system, but three are close to it—Belgium, the Federal German Republic, and Austria. In all three, an electoral reform, replacing proportional representation with a majority rule based on a single ballot, would probably result in a two-party system.

□ THE BELGIAN SYSTEM In the nineteenth century, Belgium had a two-party system as rigid as the one in Britain. A conservative Catholic party, strongly organized and closely tied to the church hierarchy, was opposed by a Liberal party, equally well disciplined. Toward the end of the century, a Socialist party developed and made progressive gains at the expense of the Liberal party. The latter began to decline, and its elimination appeared likely. The declining curve of seats held by the Belgian Liberals strongly resembles that of the British Liberals. But the Belgian conservatives united with the Liberals to replace the majority vote system with proportional representation in order to prevent the Socialists from completely supplanting the Liberals and governing by themselves (1899). From that moment on, the Liberal party ceased its decline. Or more precisely, its decline slowed down considerably, so that the Liberal party has not only succeeded in maintaining itself but has also managed to make occasional spectacular comebacks (as in the 1965 elections).

Accordingly, Belgium has an uneven three-party system with two large parties, Socialists and Social Christians, which normally receive more than four-fifths of the votes cast, and a small party that captures from 10 to 15 per cent of the votes. Therefore, we can characterize the Belgian system as "para-dualistic." But the presence of the Liberal party usually prevents either the Socialists or the Social Christians from obtaining an absolute majority (the Social Christians did manage to win a majority, however, in 1950, with 108 seats out of 212). Consequently, the government cannot generally function without a coalition. One of the unique features of Belgian political life is the fact that the country has been governed by a three-party alliance seven different times between 1918 and 1938 and between 1940 and 1949. But there have also been other combinations: a Socialist-Liberal coalition from 1954 to 1958; a Catholic-Liberal coalition from 1958 to 1965, and a Catholic-Socialist coalition today.

□ THE GERMAN SYSTEM   Before 1933, Germany had a multi-party system that was favored under the Imperial government by a parliamentary majority vote on two ballots, and under the Weimar Republic by proportional representation. The

Austria. Also, the year 1967 saw the rise of a new neo-Nazi
party, the NPD, which gained seats in several state legislatures
and picked up several seats in the national Bundestag in 1969.
There is a danger that it will gain influence if "the great coalition" persists, for the Austrian example has shown that such
a system becomes unpopular. German "para-dualism" is not
yet seriously threatened, but it is less secure. An election reform calling for the adoption of a majority vote on a single
ballot would guarantee its continuation. But the two major
parties do not intend to press for its adoption until the 1973
elections.

☐ THE AUSTRIAN SYSTEM   Austria is even closer to a two-party
system than the Federal German Republic. The two principal
parties—the Popular party (Christian Democrat) and the Socialist party—received between them more than 90 per cent of
the votes and seats in parliament. The establishment of a majority vote rule on a single ballot, which would eliminate the
third party (Liberal), is even more desirable than in Germany,
because this particular party is more demagogic and more dis-
quieting. It is closer to neo-Nazism than its German counterpart. In certain respects, the extreme right in Austria is the
most powerful in Europe, although we must be careful not to
overestimate its importance.

Until 1966, neither of the two major parties had won a majority in parliament, and it appeared as if the voters were in-
tent on keeping it this way by switching their votes whenever
one of the two parties seemed on the verge of obtaining a
majority. The Christian Democrats continue to distrust the
Socialists, whom they regard as "Reds." It is true that "Austro-
Marxism," unlike German socialism, was formerly revolutionary. For their part, the Austrian Socialists have not forgotten
that the Christian Democrats did not hesitate to direct ma-
chinegun fire into the workers' quarters during the Vienna
Commune thirty years ago, and that the Christian Democrats
supported the corporatist dictatorship of Dollfuss. To keep

each other under close surveillance, the two main parties therefore govern together, even though the coalition is beset by crises. This alliance is based on a strict distribution of government positions, ministerial posts, and other advantages between Christian Democrats and Socialists. It is the famous *proporz* (proportional) system, which is also applied to ordinary government jobs, subsidies, citations and honors, the university, and so forth, resulting in a state of political immobility. Since 1966, when they obtained an absolute parliamentary majority, the Christian Democrats have governed by themselves; but the spirit of the earlier coalition persists to a degree, and the *proporz* does too.

MULTIPARTY SYSTEMS

Except for Great Britain, West Germany, Austria, and Belgium, no European country is close to a two-party system. In no other country could an electoral reform produce a dual party system, because they are too far removed to begin with. These multiparty systems may be classified into two main categories—the Nordic types existing in Scandinavia and the Netherlands, and the Latin types which operate in France and Italy. In Scandinavia and in the Netherlands, the multiparty system shows some common traits: the parties are strongly organized and disciplined, and government coalitions are stable because the party leadership is able to enforce compliance among the membership. In France and Italy, on the other hand, the parties are less organized and less disciplined, with the result that alliances are more fragile and governments less stable.

Nordic Multiparty Systems We can consider the party systems within the four Scandinavian countries together, even though the Finnish system differs slightly from the other three, primarily because of the presence of an important Communist party. The Dutch system is substantially different. We might also add Switzerland to these Nordic multiparty systems because of the discipline and organization of its political parties; but Switzerland differs greatly in other respects, notably in its federal structure.

☐ THE SCANDINAVIAN SYSTEM The Scandinavian system is based on two fundamental elements. First, there are four main parties as the result of the development of an agrarian party alongside the conservatives, the liberals, and the socialists. Second, there is a great imbalance between these four principal parties, with the Social Democrats occupying the position of dominant party.

Nevertheless, the four-party system is quite different in each of the four Scandinavian countries. Except for Sweden, where it receives more than 15 per cent of the votes, the Liberal party is much weaker than the others (5 to 7 per cent of the votes on the average). In Norway, the Peasant party is very weak (less than 10 per cent of the votes), and in Denmark, there is no real peasant party. In Finland, there are five major parties, not four, with the Communist party winning 22 per cent of the votes, slightly more than the Socialists. Actually, Sweden is the only country that really fits the four-party system model: Finland has four large parties and one small one (Liberal); Denmark has three main parties and one small one (liberal, which calls itself Radical); Norway has two major parties and two small ones (Liberal and Peasant). Despite the differences, however, the basic pattern is discernible in all four countries.

The preponderance of the Social Democrats is very apparent, except in Finland with its division between Socialists and Communists. Yet, actually, Finland was the first country in the world where Social Democrats obtained a majority of the parliamentary seats (in 1916) and thus found themselves in a dominant position. The Communist rift put an end to this situation, but the two workers' parties together have roughly the same electoral strength as socialism has in the rest of Scandinavia. The Socialist party held an absolute majority in

Sweden from 1940 to 1944, and in Norway from 1945 to 1961. It has yet to obtain a majority in Denmark, but it has come very close to doing so. At the present time, the Socialists in Sweden, Norway, and Denmark, receive about 40 per cent of the votes cast, which is at least twice that of the party immediately behind them. Hence it is very difficult to govern without Socialist participation or support, unless all the other parties unite against them (as has been the case in Norway since 1966, and in Denmark since 1968). Their size gives them a predominant influence within party alliances and throughout each country. Just as people used to talk about the radical republic of France before 1936, today they talk about the socialist monarchies in Scandinavia.

☐ THE DUTCH SYSTEM The party system in the Netherlands is characterized by the close ties between politics and religion. We have indicated how these ties led to a three-way split among the conservatives—one group Catholic and the other two, the Anti-Revolutionary party and the Historical Christian party, Protestant (the differences between these two are religious as well as political, for the Historical Christians correspond to a particular interpretation of Protestantism). But, except perhaps for the Liberals, the other parties also have certain religious characteristics. The case of the Socialist party is very interesting in this connection. The Labor party, founded in 1946, is a new version of the old Social Democratic party, which even formed the nucleus of the new party after renouncing Marxist and materialist doctrines. It was joined by the Dutch Popular Movement, a party with both socialist and Christian (but nondenominational tendencies).

Moreover, the Catholics are less conservative than the Protestant Anti-Revolutionary and Historical Christian parties. They have a tradition of forming coalitions with the left. In the nineteenth century, they governed for a long time in cooperation with the Liberals. Today they do not hesitate to form alliances with the Socialists. Thus they play the role of a center party, tipping the political scales one way or the other. From 1946 to 1959, the Netherlands was governed by a Catholic-Socialist coalition, which was followed by a Catholic-Protestant coalition. Dutch alliances vary considerably, which is explained by the fact that no party is dominant (the Catholics and the Socialists are stronger than the others, but neither party can count on winning one-third of the electorate). Yet once established, Dutch coalition governments remain stable for a long time. Consequently, putting a coalition together is generally a laborious task. Ministerial crises are rare in the Netherlands, but when they occur, they last a long time. Forming a new ministry, after the fall of its predecessor or at the beginning of a new legislative session, is always very difficult, for it requires the most detailed and carefully planned adjustments. The process usually takes a month or more.

Multiparty Systems in the South   To contrast the Nordic and Latin multiparty systems suggests that we are referring to the old theories of Montesquieu regarding the influence of climate upon man—theories that are still current to some extent among the general public: Nordics are wise and disciplined by nature; Latins are undisciplined, capricious, and impulsive. The classification we propose has nothing to do with these alleged political "temperaments," but is simply based on the fact that political parties in the north are better organized, more rigid, and more cohesive than those in the south. Nevertheless, we must not exaggerate this contrast: the French and Italian Communist parties are more strongly organized than any Dutch or Scandinavian political party. Also, there is a great difference between the structure of French parties and Italian parties.

☐ THE ITALIAN SYSTEM   Italian political parties are rather well organized. The Communist party there is the most powerful in the Western world. Although it allows more freedom of discussion than any other communist party, discipline is rigid and the organization is well regulated. The Chirstian Democratic party is not so well disciplined because its membership includes groups with differing tendencies, from the right to the center left. But these tendencies are taken into account by a system of proportional representation in the party congresses. The membership is large and well organized. And finally, the Italian Christian Democratic party is more highly structured than Scandinavian or Dutch parties of the political right, or than the British Conservative party. However, great organizational weakness is found in the socialist parties, so dissimilar in this respect to their counterparts in the north. Lacking the support of labor unions spawned by anarcho-syndicalism, Italian socialism has always been rather weak, like French socialism. Since 1945, it has become even weaker through internal dissension. At the time of the Liberation, there were two rival socialist parties: the Italian Socialist party of Pietro Nenni, who collaborated with the communists, and the Social Democratic party of Giuseppe Saragat. Thereafter, the Italian Socialist party severed its ties with the Communist party to collaborate with the Christian Democrats, the Social Democrats, and the small secular parties (Liberals and Republicans) and form a majority of the center left. This produced a split with its left-wing elements, who formed the Italian Socialist Party of Proletarian Unity (the PSIUP). In October 1966, the PSI and the Social Democratic party merged.

Italy is characterized, above all, by a very large number of political parties. It has a Communist party, two socialist parties (three before 1966), two small, nonclerical liberal parties (Republicans and Liberals), the Christian Democratic party, and also two parties on the far right (the neo-fascist Italian Social Movement and the Monarchist party; at one time there were even two monarchist parties, one of which was maintained in Naples by the powerful shipbuilder, Lauro). This makes a total of eight parties represented in parliament, without mentioning some tiny groups with no electoral bases or the Tyrolean Autonomy party. If we remember that the Christian Democrats are a federation of heterogeneous groups rather than a truly unified party, we can see that the Italian political spectrum represents many shades of opinion.

This great multiplicity of parties has created fewer problems than one might expect, because of the imbalance in their size and strength and the dominant character of the Christian Democratic party, which, alone, continues to receive a third of the votes cast during national elections. From 1948 to 1953, it held an absolute majority of the seats in parliament (305 out of 590) and was able to govern effectively. The situation has changed since 1953, and Italian governments are dependent upon coalitions. But the Christian Democrats remain the pivotal party: the others are too numerous and too weak to form an alliance against them. The chief difficulty lies in the internal divisions among the Christian Democrats. Since 1946, the party has moved steadily to the right, and the proportion of conservatives has grown steadily. Despite this trend, the left-wing of the party refuses to form any rightist coalition with the neo-fascists or the monarchists. The center maneuvers between the two groups. At the present moment, Italy is ruled by a majority with a so-called "opening to the left," which groups the small secular parties around the Christian Democrats and the moderate socialists.

Counterbalancing the Christian Democrats are the Communist and socialist parties. In 1963, the Communists elected 166 deputies, and the socialist parties elected a total of 120. The overall strength of the socialists (286 deputies), is greater than that of the Christian Democratic party, and if they were unified, they would have a very good chance of securing an absolute parliamentary majority. This explains the efforts of the Italian Communist party to reach an agreement with the socialists. The Communists have gone so far as to propose dissolving their party in order to establish a Unified Workers' party. But the socialists are not inclined to accept such a proposal, or even to form a simple alliance with the Communists. The Italian Socialist party of Pietro Nenni formed an alliance of this kind—a very close alliance—from 1950 to 1956, and it does not want to do so again. It prefers, instead, to seek an alliance and eventually a merger with the Social Democratic party. Fear of communism, which results in keeping the Communist party isolated, thus aggravates Italy's political divisions and makes it more difficult to establish stable parliamentary majorities. Because of this fear, the formation of a majority on the left is still out of the question.

□ THE FRENCH SYSTEM   The French party system resembles the Italian—numerous parties, weak internal organization, and the presence of a strong Communist party. However, there are several fundamental differences, which have been accentuated by recent political developments.

In the first place, there are seven parties in France, as compared with nine in the Italian peninsula: the Democratic Union for the Fifth Republic (formerly the UNR), the Independent Republicans, the Democratic Center, the Radicals, the Socialist party (the SFIO), the Unified Socialist party (still very small), and the Communist party. In the second place, French parties are more loosely organized, less disciplined, and less powerful than the Italian parties. Only the two communist parties are comparable, even though the Italian Communist party is stronger and more dynamic. The French socialist parties are much weaker than their Italian counterparts. The Democratic Center and the Independent Republicans are made up of electoral committees including a few prominent citizens, and are united by a very weak central organization: they can hardly be compared with the powerful Italian Christian Democratic party. Even the UDV^e (Democratic Union for the Fifth Republic) has a fairly weak party apparatus and does not seek a mass membership.

The characteristic feature of French parties is their extraordinary weakness. Only the Communists have a large party membership—500,000, they say, but it is probably between 250,000 and 300,000. Though half the size of the Italian Communist party, it is still very large as French parties go. The French Socialist party claims 90,000 members; it is more likely 50,000–60,000. The German Socialist party has 620,000; the Austrian Socialist party, 710,000; the Swedish Socialist party, 800,000; and the British Labour party has 5,500,000 indirect members (through the Trade Unions) and 750,000 regular members. Other French parties are skeletal in size: the Unified Socialist party (PSU) does not have 20,000 members; the Radicals and Independents can muster only a few thousand throughout the entire country. Only the UDV^e seems to have a somewhat larger membership. This situation is not altogether new. French political parties have always been of a traditional nature, built around small cadres, rather than parties of the masses, but never have conditions been quite so serious. In 1946, the Communist party had nearly a million members and the Socialists more than 350,000. During the Third Republic [1870–1940], the Radical party included a large number of locally prominent citizens who were in contact with public opinion. The unpopularity of present-day French parties is mostly due to this weakness. We cannot regard them as representing the country's major political tendencies when they shrivel up and congeal in their ancient, outmoded political apparatus. Nevertheless, the development of the UDV^e on the right, and of the Democratic and Socialist Federation on the left, marks a beginning in the opposite direction.

A third feature distinguishes the French party system from the Italian: in France, no one party is dominant like the Christian Democratic party in Italy. However, at the present moment, the UDV^e occupies a very strong position and has apparently managed to put down strong organizational roots that have enabled it to survive the disappearance of its charismatic founder, General de Gaulle. It is opposed on the left by a shifting coalition of parties, including the Communists, Socialists, and other small parties.

Since the presidential election of 1965, French political parties have been moving even further away from the Italian example and closer to a dual party system. The old *Mouvement Républicain Populaire* (which was Christian Democratic) has disappeared to become the nucleus of the Democratic Center, in which we find a regrouping of non-Gaullist Independents and old-line Radicals, who were opposed to their party's movement toward the left. The Independent Republicans have been closely allied to the UDV[e], since they presented a common slate of candidates for the legislative elections of 1967. Together they form the present ruling majority of the French government. The Radicals and French Socialists have united within the Federation of the Democratic and Socialist Left, which is expected to become a unified party in 1969. Consequently, there are no more than five parliamentary groups in the present National Assembly: the UDV[e], the Independent Republicans, the Democratic Center ("Modern Progress and Democracy"), the Federation, and the Communist party.

Moreover, the alliance between the Federation and the Communist party in the 1965 presidential elections and the 1967 legislative elections brought the Communists out of their isolation. In this respect, the French situation became quite different from the Italian, which it had resembled from 1947 to 1965. Instead, it resembled the situation in France before 1939. Under the Third Republic, two main coalitions competed during national elections and more or less alternated with each other in running the government: the coalition of the left— the *Bloc* of 1902, 1906, and 1914; the Cartel of 1924, 1928, and 1932; the Popular Front in 1936—and the coalition of the right, the *Bloc National*. Between 1947 and 1965, a split in the left, almost evenly divided between Communists and noncommunists, prevented a continuation of this political strategy. Then, only majorities of the right or of the center were possible. But with the alliance of the Federation of the Democratic and Socialist Left and the Communist party it once more became possible to form a parliamentary majority and support a government of the left, including Communist ministers (only 24 per cent of the French electorate were opposed to such a possibility according to a public opinion poll taken in December 1966, 40 per cent approved, 27 per cent had no opinion, and 9 per cent declined to answer).

Accordingly, French political forces are moving in the direction of a "bipolarization." Faced with a coalition of the right, including the UDV^e and Independent Republicans (with 38 per cent of the votes cast in the 1967 elections), a coalition of the left is developing, including the Federation, the Communists, and the Unified Socialist party, which won a combined total of 43.5 per cent of the votes in 1967. Between these two coalitions, the Democratic Center has lost strength, receiving only 17.8 per cent of the votes in 1967 (this figure also includes the votes for certain uncommitted candidates, some of whom rallied to the majority). Consequently, it is much easier to form a stable parliamentary majority than it was from 1947 to 1958. As a matter of fact, such a majority has existed since 1962, and it is now possible for the opposition on the left to establish a majority of its own. The constitutional reform of 1962 played an important role in this connection: the election of the president of the Republic by universal suffrage provided the principal instrument for the regrouping of parties that has since occurred. The regrouping also reflects a fundamental change in French society (see bibliography that follows).

BIBLIOGRAPHY

Concerning political parties in present-day Europe, see P. Lalumière and A. Demichel, *Les régimes parlementaires européens,* 1966. On their historical development, see Charles Seignobos, *Histoire politique de l'Europe contemporaine (1814–1914),* 2d ed., 1924; G. Weill, *L'Europe du XIXe siècle et l'idée de nationalité,* 1938; R. Schnerb, *Le XIXe siècle,* 1955 (in the "Histoire Générale des Civilisations" under the general editorship of M. Crouzet, vol. VI); the works in the collection "Peuples et Civilisations": G. Weill, *L'éveil des na-*

tionalités et le mouvement libéral (1815–1848), 1930; C. Pouthas, *Démocraties et capitalisme (1848–1860)*, 2d ed., 1948; M. Hauser, J. Maurain, P. Benaerts, F. L'Huillier, *Du libéralisme à l'impéralisme* (1860–1878), 1952; M. Baumont, *L'essor industriel et l'impéralisme colonial*, 2d ed., 1949.

The most important work on political ideologies is J. Bowle, *Politics and Opinion in the Nineteenth Century*, London, 1954; see also J. Touchard et al., *Histoire des idées politiques*, 3d ed., 1965; F. Ponteil, *La pensée politique depuis Montesquieu*, 1960. Concerning liberalism, see G. de Ruggiero, *Storia del liberalismo europeo*, 5th ed., Bari, 1949; G. Weill, *Histoire du Parti républicain en France de 1814 à 1870*, 1900. Concerning conservatism, see R. Rémond, *La droite en France, de la Restauration à la Ve République*, 2d ed., 1964; *Les idées traditionalistes en France de Rivarol à Charles Maurras*, Urbana. Ill., 1937; R. J. Whibe, *The Conservative Tradition*, London, 1950.

Concerning socialism, see J. Droz, *Le socialisme démocratique*, 1967; G. D. H. Cole, *Socialist Thought*, London, 5 vols., 1953–1960; E. Halévy, *Histoire du socialisme européen*, 1948; M. Leroy, *Histoire des idées sociales en France*, 3 vols., 1946–1950; L. Valiani, *Histoire du socialisme au XXe siècle*, 1948; C. A. Landauer, *European Socialism*, Berkeley, Calif., 1959. Concerning Christian Democracy, see R. Aubert, J.-B. Duroselle, and A. Jemold, "Le libéralisme religieux au XIXe siècle" in the *Actes du Xe Congrès des Sciences historiques de Rome* (September 1955), vol. V, pp. 303–383; J.-B. Duroselle, *Les débats du catholicisme social en France* (1822–1870), 1951; W. Gurian, *Die politischen und sozialen Ideen des französischen Katholicismus (1789–1914)*, Munich, 1929; M. Vaussard, *Histoire de la démocratie chrétienne (France, Belgique, Italie)*, 1956; M. P. Fogarty, *Christian Democracy in Western Europe*, 1957; and M. Einaudi and F. Goguel, *Christian Democracy in Italy and France*, University of Notre Dame, Indiana, 1952.

Concerning fascism, see G. J. Friedrich and L. K. Brezezinski, *Totalitarian Dictatorship and Autocracy*, Cambridge, Mass., 1956; W. M. McGovern, *From Luther to Hitler: The History of Fascist-Nazi Philosophy*, Boston, 1950; and H. Arendt, *The Origins of Totalitarianism*, New York, 1951.

Concerning political parties in France, see F. Goguel and A. Grosser, *La politique en France*, 1964; M. Duverger et al., *Partis politiques et classes sociales,* 1955; M. Duverger, "Public Opinion and Political Parties in France," *American Political Science Review* (1952), pp. 1069ff.; F. Goguel, *La politique des partis sous la IIIᵉ République,* 2d ed., 1958; J. Fauvet, *Les partis politiques dans la France actuelle,* 1947, and *La France déchirée,* 1957; the special issue of *Esprit,* May 1939, on "Le régime des partis": P. Marabuto, *Les partis politiques et les mouvements sociaux sous la IVᵉ République,* 1948; A. Siegfried, *Tableau des partis en France,* 1930, and *Tableau politique de la France de l'Ouest sous la IIIᵉ République,* 1913; the brief study by J. Malterre and P. Benoist, *Les partis politiques français,* 1956; see also E. Mead Earle et al., *Modern France,* Princeton, 1951; P. Williams, *Politics in Post-War France,* London, 2d ed., 1956; and especially the very interesting collective study, *Tendances politiques dans la vie française depuis 1789* ("*Colloques,*" *Cahiers de civilisation*), and *A la recherche de la France,* 1963 (trans. from the English). Concerning the present crisis in French parties, see G. Vedel et al., *La dépolitisation: mythe ou réalité?,* 1962; and the chronicles on French political forces published by the *Revue française de Science politique,* since 1963.

Concerning conservative parties, see René Remond, *La droite en France, de la Restauration à la Vᵉ République,* 2d ed., 1964; A. Dansette, *Histoire religieuse de la France contemporaine,* vol. II, 1948–1951, and *Destin du catholicisme française (1926–1956),* 1957; J. Charlot, *L'U.N.R.: étude du pouvoir au sein d'un parti politique,* 1967; C. Purtschet, *Le Rassemblement du peuple français (1947–1953),* 1965; S. Hoffmann, *Le mouvement Poujade,* 1956 (concerning Poujadism, see also the bibliography and chronological commentary of J. Touchard in the *Revue française de Science politique,* 1958, p. 18; one should also read the picturesque *Mein Kampf* of Pierre Poujade, *J'ai choisi le combat,* Saint-Céré, 1955). Concerning the extreme right, see G. Girardet, *"L'Héritage de l'Action française"* (French trans.), 1964; E. R. Tannenbaum, *The Action Française,* New York, 1962, and J. Plumyène and R. Lasierra, *Les fascismes français (1923–1963),* 1963; S. M. Osgood, *French Royalism under the Third and Fourth Republics,* The Hague, 1960.

Concerning liberalism and the Radical party, see C. Nicolet, *Le radicalisme,* 1957; D. Bardonnet, *L'évolution de la structure du Parti radical,* 1960; F. de Tarr, *The French Radical Party,* London, 1961; J. Kayser, *Les grandes batailles du radicalisme (1820–1901),*

1962; J. A. Scott, *Republican Ideas and the Liberal Tradition in France (1870–1914)*, New York, 1951; Alain (Emile Chartier), *Eléments d'une doctrine radicale,* reprinted in 1933 (an essential document on the radical state of mind as it was at the beginning of the century); D. Halévy, *La République des Comités,* 1934; M. Sorre, "Les pères du radicalisme," *Rev. fr. de Sci. pol.* (1951), p. 481; A. Milhaud, *Histoire du radicalisme,* 1951; F. Buisson, *La politique radicale,* 1908. Concerning the M.R.P. and Christian Democracy, see the writings of M. Vaussard, M. Einaudi, F. Goguel, and M. P. Fogarty, mentioned above, and L. Biton, *La démocratie chrétienne dans la politique française,* Angers, 1954; R. Havard De La Montagne, *Histoire de la démocratie chrétienne, de Lamennais à Georges Bidault,* 1948; and the interesting work by G. Suffert, *Les catholiques et la gauche,* 1960.

Concerning socialist parties, see D. Ligou, *Histoire du socialisme en France* (1871–1961), 1962; G. Lefranc, *Le mouvement socialiste sous la IIIe République,* 1963; the special issue of *Esprit,* May 1956; M. Duverger, "S.F.I.O.: mort ou transfiguration?" in the special issue of the review, *Les Temps Modernes* (May 1955), pp. 383ff., and "Néo-socialisme 1957," *Le Monde,* July 11 and 12, 1947; G. Nania, *Un parti de la gauche: le P.S.U.,* 1966; A. Philip, *Le socialisme trahi,* 1957, and *Pour un socialisme humaniste,* 1960; E. Depreux, *Le renouvellement du socialisme,* 1960; J. Moch, *Socialisme vivant,* 1960; M. Prélot, *L'évolution politique du socialisme français,* 1939; J. T. Marcus, *French Socialism in the Crisis Years 1933–1936,* London, 1958; P. Louis, *Le Parti socialiste en France,* vol. I of *L'Encyclopédie socialiste, syndicale et coopérative,* 1912. Concerning the origins of the French Socialist party [the SFIO—Section Française de l'Internationale Ouvrière], see A. Noland, *The Founding of the French Socialist Party,* 1893–1905, Cambridge, Mass., 1956; J. J. Fiechter, *Le socialisme français, de l'Affaire Dreyfus à la Grande Guerre,* Geneva, 1965.

Concerning the Communist party, see G. Walter, *Histoire du Parti communiste français,* 1948; A. Kriegel, *Aux origines du communisme français (1914–1920),* 2 vols., 1964; and *Le Congrès de Tours,* 1964; J. Fauvet, *Histoire du Parti communiste français,* 2 vols., 1964–1966; M. Einaudi, J. M. Domenach, and A. Garosci, *Communism in Western Europe,* Ithaca, N.Y., 1951; C. A. Micaud, *Communism and the French Left,* New York, 1963; H. Lefebvre, *La somme et le reste,*

2 vols., 1958; A. Brayanke, *Anatomie du Parti communiste français,* 1953; A. J. Rieber, *Stalin and the French Communist Party (1941– 1947),* New York, 1962; and the Communist party's publications, especially the collection of *Cahiers du Communisme.* Concerning the party's crisis since "de-Stalinization," see J. Baby, *Critique de base,* 1960; J. Touchard, "De l'affaire Lecoeur à l'affaire Hervé," *Rev. fr. de Sci. pol.* (1956), pp. 388ff., with bibliography, and especially J. Dru, *Le Parti démocratique,* 1963.

Concerninp political parties in Great Britain, see R. T. Mac-Kenzie, *British Political Parties,* London, 2d ed., 1963; Sir Ivor Jennings, *Party Politics,* 3 vols., Cambridge: vol. I, *Appeal to the People,* 1960; vol. II, *The Growth of Parties,* 1961; vol. III, *The Stuff of Politics,* 1962; I. Bulmer-Thomas, *The Party System in Great Britain,* London, 1952; A. H. Birch, P. W. Campbell, W. J. M. Mac-Kenzie, "Partis politiques et classes sociales en Angleterre," *Rev. Fr. de Sci. pol.* (1955), p. 772. Concerning parties in the Federal German Republic, see F. A. F. Von der Heydte and K. Sacherl, *Soziologie der Deutschen Parteien,* Munich, 1955; M. G. Lance, G. Schulz, and K. Schutz, *Parteien in der Bundesrepublik,* Stuttgart, 1955; O. K. Flechtheim, *Die Deutschen Parteien seit 1945,* 3 vols., Berlin, 1955– 1963; J. Rovan, *Le catholicisme politique en Allemagne,* 1956; D. A. Chalmers, *The Social Democratic Party of Germany,* New Haven, Conn., and London, 1964; J. Pirker, *Die S.P.D. nach Hitler,* Munich, 1965; the article by A. J. Heidenheimer on the C.D.U. [Christian Democratic Union] in *Rev. Fr. de Sci. pol.* (1957), p. 626. Concerning parties in Italy, see J.-P. Chasseriaud, *Le Parti démocrate-chrétien en Italie,* 1965; T. Godechot, *Le Parti démocrate-chrétien italien,* 1964; M. Einaudi, J. M. Domenach, and A. Garosci, *Communism in Western Europe,* Ithaca, N.Y., 1951; G. Candeloro, *Il movimento cattólico in Italia,* 1955; F. Magri, *La democrazia cristiana in Italia,* 2 vols., 1954–55; and the works of M. Einaudi and M. P. Fogarty given herein. Concerning parties in Scandinavia, see R. Fusilier, *Le Parti socialiste suédois,* 1964, and *Les Pays nordiques,* 1965; D. Philip, *Le mouvement ouvrier en Norvège,* 1958; H. Valen and D. Katz, *Political Parties in Norway,* Oslo, 1966. Concerning parties in Belgium, see A. Melot, *Le Parti catholique en Belgique,* Louvain, 1934; E. Vandervelde, *Le Parti ouvrier belge de 1885 à 1925,* Brussels, 1925; M. A. Pierson, *Histoire du socialisme en Bel-*

gique, Brussels, 1953; R. de Smet, and R. Evalenko, *Les élections belges,* Brussels, 1956; *Les élections législatives belges de 1958,* Brussels, 1959; and the study by M. Vaussard, mentioned previously. Concerning parties in Switzerland, see F. Masnata, *Le Parti socialiste et la tradition démocratique en Suisse,* 1964.

The underlying causes of changes in French political parties since 1965 are analyzed in M. Duverger, *La démocratie sans le peuple,* 1967, in which is set forth a system explaining the political evolution of France since 1789. Concerning the evolution itself, one should also consult: R. Barrillon, *La gauche française en mouvement,* 1967; the special issue of the journal *France-Forum,* "La France va-t-elle au bipartisme?" (June 1967); the article by F. Goguel in *Revue Française de Science Politique* (1967), p. 918, and the debates sponsored by the Association Française de Science Politique: *"Le bipartisme est-il possible en France?"* (Introduction by M. Duverger and J. Fauvet), 1965 (mimeographed), and *"Permanence et changement dans le système des partis français"* (Introduction by M. Duverger and F. Goguel, 1967 [mimeographed]).

The present movement toward bipolarization was prompted by the 1965 presidential election and by certain other technical factors (the need for the left to unite to counterbalance Gaullism, the replacement of proportional representation by a majority ballot for legislative elections). But it is essentially the result of a deep-seated change in French society. In order for a dual political system to function, each party (or coalition of parties) must not fear that its opponent will abuse its power when in control of the government. This change of attitude is not possible so long as extremist elements dominate the political scene—a fact which indicates that social tensions are very acute. Such was the situation in France throughout the nineteenth century and the beginning of the twentieth, and this produced "centrism."

Economic developments and the growth of a consumer society have changed the basic elements of the problem. Social antagonisms have not disappeared, but they are becoming less violent. Hence the extreme right has almost completely disappeared. As for the communist extreme left, it, too, is undergoing a change. It is becoming progressively less extreme, less revolutionary. The Communist party continues to yearn for the establishment of a new social order, but it hardly envisages the use of force any longer to achieve its objective. Consequently, it is now possible to have coalition governments of the right (like the present one in power since 1962) alternate in power with coalition governments of the left (like the one being put together by the Federation and the Communists).

□ PART TWO □

PRESSURE GROUPS

Political parties strive to acquire power and to exercise it—by electing town councilors, local officials, mayors, senators, and deputies, and by choosing cabinet ministers and the head of state. Pressure groups, on the contrary, do not participate directly in the acquisition of power or in its exercise; they act to influence power while remaining apart from it; they exert "pressure" on it (whence their name, which we introduced into France some ten years ago as a direct translation of the American expression "pressure groups"). Pressure groups seek to influence the men who wield power, not to place their own men in power, at least not officially. However, certain powerful groups actually have their own representatives in governments and legislative bodies, but the relationship between these individuals and the groups they represent remains secret or circumspect.

Pressure groups are less easily classified than political parties. Parties are organizations exclusively concerned with political action; they are simply political parties. Most pressure groups, on the other hand, are nonpolitical organizations, and political pressure is not their primary activity. Any group, association, or organization, even those whose normal concerns are far removed from politics, can act as a pressure group in certain areas and under certain circumstances.

□ 3 □

THE GENERAL THEORY
OF PRESSURE GROUPS

First providing a more precise definition of pressure groups, we shall then outline their organization and activity. This outline, based on a comparative observation of the facts and not on *a priori* reasoning, sets out to describe the framework, enabling one to proceed further with a concrete analysis of the various pressure groups.

THE IDEA OF "PRESSURE GROUP"

We have just defined a pressure group by comparing it with a political party. But we must also define it with respect to nonpolitical organizations, that are neither parties nor pressure groups. This second definition is much less precise inasmuch as any organization, as we have already indicated, can behave like a pressure group under certain conditions and in certain areas. This question is the first that needs clarification.

Then, we shall attempt to distinguish genuine pressure groups from pseudopressure groups.

PRESSURE GROUPS DEFINED

Two basic problems arise in this connection: are organizations with only a few activities in the area of political pressure to be considered pressure groups; and can governmental groups be pressure groups, or should this concept apply only to "private groups"?

Exclusive Groups and Partial Groups   While clear in principle, this distinction is not so clear in its application.

A pressure group is "exclusive" if it is solely concerned with taking action in the political domain, with bringing pressure to bear upon public power. Such, for example, is the French Parliamentary Association for the Defense of Educational Freedom and the famous lobbies in Washington, D.C., organizations that specialize in intervening with senators and congressmen, with cabinet members and other high government officials. A group is "partial," on the other hand, if political pressure is only one facet of its activities, if it has other reasons for its existence and other means of action. Such, for instance, is a labor union that occasionally exerts pressure on the government, but is primarily concerned with broader objectives. "Partial" groups are plentiful. As we have stated, any group or any organization may be induced to exert political pressure at some time in the course of its activities. The French Academy has sometimes intervened to try to limit government taxes imposed on books and writers. Churches are not above exerting pressure on public authorities, any more than philosophical associations, cultural societies, and intellectual groups.

In practice, the distinction between the two types of groups is not always easy to apply. Certain "exclusive" groups are in fact only technical agencies acting on behalf of other groups which are "partial." The lobbies in Washington, D.C., are, more and more, becoming specialized agencies that can be hired by any group with the means to pay for them. They are somewhat like tax consultants or legal advisers. The real pressure comes from those who make use of the lobbies, not from the lobbies themselves. Moreover, exclusive groups almost always attempt to conceal their true activity behind supposedly lofty objectives. They represent a particular example of a much broader political phenomenon that we have previously discussed—camouflage. Since the public in general takes a rather dim view of pressure groups and their activities, exclusive pressure groups seldom admit their true nature and try to project the image of an organization having much broader, more prestigious goals. In other words, they try to appear as partial groups to the public.

Finally, more important than distinguishing between "partial" groups and "exclusive" groups is determining the exact place that pressure activities hold in the partial groups, because the true exclusive groups are, after all, very rare. For some groups, political pressure is an occasional and an exceptional activity. Such is the case with the French Academy protesting the amount of taxes levied on books and authors. At the other extreme, alongside the self-proclaimed exclusive groups (such as the French Parliamentary Association for Academic Freedom), there are groups that are virtually exclusive despite their efforts to appear otherwise, such as the French Association for the Defense of Free Enterprise. Between these two extremes, we find a wide range of intermediate situations.

Hence it is not possible to restrict our notion of a pressure group to organizations that engage exclusively or primarily in the exercise of political pressure, for these groups are not clearly distinguishable from organizations whose pressure activities are more limited. Nor is it possible to exclude from the category of pressure groups organizations that engage in pressure tactics very infrequently. Here again, no demarcation line can be drawn. Keeping these reservations in mind, when we draw up a list of pressure groups, we are referring above all to organizations and associations in which pressure activities play an important role within each group. The fact remains that we cannot provide a complete list of a country's pressure groups in the same manner that we can provide a complete list of its political parties.

Private Groups and Public Groups The idea of pressure groups was first developed in the United States where it served as a basis for studying the actions and influence of private groups and organizations on public power. At first, the idea of pressure groups referred only to "private" groups, but there is a growing tendency to expand the concept to include public agencies and governmental bodies, which is to say, "public" groups.

It was recognized that public agencies sometimes behave very much like pressure groups. The legal principle of the unity of the state hardly corresponds to reality. The various governmental agencies are usually engaged in bitter rivalries for influence in determining governmental policies. In this struggle, each of them acts more or less like a pressure group with respect to the government and the legislature. Accordingly, their behavior invites comparison with that of private groups, on which the original concept of pressure groups is based.

We can discern two kinds of public groups. The first conforms to the example we have just given—official agencies of government acting like pressure groups to defend the interests of their agencies, which, moreover, they tend to identify with the public interest. The second type is made up of government officials who constitute a kind of secret fraternity, hoping to monopolize the top administrative posts and positions of influence. In France, we find this type, for example, in the Treasury Department, the Council of State, the Department of Mines, and among fellow alumni of the *Ecole Polytechnique*.[1]

[1] A prestigious French school of science and engineering.

While the emphasis on one's personal career is of great importance, there is in addition a group or corporative interest, also identified with the public interest, that frequently predominates.

However, the distinction between public groups and private groups is far from clear, for the general development of modern states tend to blur it. Many private groups actually play a public role. Are not most of them really "semipublic" groups? In certain governmental agencies, private influences are very noticeable, such as the Department of Agriculture, the Merchant Marine, or Industrial Production. Rather than a qualitative difference between two sharply defined categories, there are differences of degree reflecting a wide range of varied categories. Public groups are at one end of the scale, and private groups are at the other, while most individual groups are situated somewhere in between.

The idea of public pressure groups offends traditional theorists, for whom, the unity of the state's organization is a sacrosanct dogma. They regard the tendency of state agencies to form pressure groups as a pathological phenomenon, symptomatic of a serious government crisis. Hence, they consider public pressure groups to be unusual and abnormal; only private groups should be considered "true" pressure groups. Nevertheless, the tendency to form public pressure groups is a general and constant phenomenon. In political sociology, the notion of public pressure groups is a very productive one. It is particularly useful in shedding light on the problem of competition in States having only one political party. When competition is eliminated on the party level, it persists within the various elements of the state which become, in fact, public pressure groups.

Foreign Pressure Groups The distinction between public and private pressure groups may be applied to national groups. Foreign pressure groups can intervene, and indeed do so effectively, in the internal political life of many countries. In their country of origin, these groups may be private or public. Thus, English labor unions that assist Italian labor unions in strike actions, or American business organizations that seek to influence French agencies, are private groups in Great Britain or in the United States. But if, on the other hand, the United States State Department intervenes with a Latin American government, or the Central Intelligence Agency influences military personnel in the Middle East, these are actions by public groups in the United States. However, for the nation that is subjected to such pressure, all these groups are private since they are foreign to its own government. It is the same when pressure is exerted by international public organizations —Common Market commissions, the European Coal and Steel Community, the Organization of American States, Comecon, and so on.

Here again, the distinction between public groups and private groups is difficult to apply. If there are ties between the national government and the foreign government whose agency is exerting the pressure, the situation takes on aspects of public pressure. The same is true if the pressure comes from an international organization when the state, which is under pressure, is a member of the organization. These pressures coming from foreign public organizations establish genuine and concrete ties of dependency and subordination between one government and another—ties that strengthen and reinforce the official dependencies and subordinations that result from commitments made through treaties and other international agreements. Or else they may establish a *de facto* dependency behind a façade of legal independence. Pressures from private foreign groups also reinforce or establish a kind of *de facto* dependency. But it is not a dependency of one government upon another; it is a dependency of a foreign government on a private organization.

PSEUDOPRESSURE GROUPS

We apply the term "pseudopressure groups" to organizations that exercise political pressure, but do not, properly speaking, constitute pressure groups. They include a certain number of individuals who, taken together, form a community. But these individuals are technicians and experts, who do not always work for themselves but on behalf of others. This definition includes two main types of organizations—technical pressure groups and the information media.

Technical Pressure Groups In a certain sense, these are purely technical organizations, not corresponding to any social community except the one provided by the organization's own experts. One may hesitate to classify them as pressure groups, for while they indeed apply "pressure," they are not, strictly speaking, "groups."

□ ELECTION CAMPAIGN FUNDS A good example is provided by the fund-raising methods for political campaigns, which are highly developed in most Western countries. The financing of elections is one of the means by which various groups bring pressure to bear on political and governmental power. This is especially true of business employers' associations. Certain business organizations pay funds directly to the candidates or to their parties. Sometimes employers' associations set up a special organization, a campaign committee, to collect contributions and assessments from various companies in proportion to their size and importance. This special group assumes responsibility for the distribution of these funds. Such a system assures greater discretion—an important consideration under the circumstances. The true function of this special agency is more or less concealed beneath an official designation as a study group or research committee. (The Union of Economic Interests of the famous Senator Billiet played this role during the Third Republic; and an organization operated by Senator Boutemy succeeded it under the Fourth Republic.) These campaign committees are unquestionably pressure groups, for they do not finance all parties indiscriminately, but only those endorsed by their contributors. They have very definite political preferences. They link together a particular group of people—the financial contributors—who wish to exert political pressure, giving them greater influence than if they acted separately. This corresponds precisely to the notion of what constitutes a pressure group.

□ LOBBIES The famous American lobbies fit more clearly into the category of technical pressure groups. Indeed, the theory of pressure groups, as developed in the United States, was based in part on the role of these political lobbies. The word "lobby" means "hall" or "corridor" and referred to the halls of Congress and other governmental offices. Lobbies are organizations that haunt the legislative hallways to "buttonhole" politicians and high government officials. Originally, these actions were undertaken by representatives of the various pressure groups themselves. Gradually, however, separate agencies were formed that specialized in lobbying and offered their services for a fee to anyone interested. To be sure, some groups retain their own organization and their own methods of pressuring politicians.

If the lobby is simply an organization of experts, like a panel of lawyers or an advertising agency, which rents its services to anyone without regard to political or social views of those who want the lobby to act on their behalf, we are not dealing with a pressure group in the proper sense of the term, but with a commercial organization that pressure groups can use to promote their own ends. The situation is different if the lobby has its own political or social orientation, if it makes its services available only to those groups who share its views and refuses to assist other groups. Under these circumstances, the lobby constitutes a genuine pressure group.

□ PRIVATE PROPAGANDA BUREAUS The same distinction applies to private propaganda bureaus, such as the Propaganda Center for National Republicans, founded in France in the 1930's by Henri de Kérillis. The center distributed posters, brochures, and political tracts to parties and candidates requesting them. Its activities thus amounted to an indirect type of financial support; instead of giving money outright, the bureau provided propaganda assistance "in kind." Such organizations assume that political parties are weak, which was the case in France for the parties on the right, the sector to which the de Kérillis organization directed its propaganda.

We should point out that private propaganda operations of this sort, specializing in a particular political sector, are tending to disappear. More and more, political parties and pressure groups are turning to the services of advertising agencies and public relations firms—enterprises that are strictly neutral and of a purely technical nature. Accordingly, they are in no sense pressure groups. But Mr. de Kérillis's Propaganda Center must still be considered a pressure group because it was more than a technical organization. Its members had a political commitment and engaged in pressure tactics only for those sharing their personal views and attitudes. The same distinction applies to lobbies. When they consist simply of experts in propaganda techniques, they are instruments used by pressure groups and are not in themselves pressure groups.

Newspapers and Information Media In a certain sense, newspapers and information media (radio and television) can be included among the pseudopressure groups. They are indeed organizations of technical experts exerting political pressure, although certain distinctions must be made in regard to them.

Some newspapers and information media do not act like pressure groups, being simply business enterprises established to make money. They sell newspapers, radio programs, and television shows in the same manner that others sell foodstuffs or men's wear. By their very nature, the press, radio, and television in capitalist societies fit into this category. They are political or educational only to the extent that they are not totally capitalistic—which is to say, only to the extent that their managers are willing to sacrifice financial gain, or even lose money, in order to influence the government or public opinion.

Newspapers and information media in capitalist countries do not seek to exert any pressure of their own. On the contrary, it is to the extent that they do not disturb the public—that they do not "pressure" it in any way—that they increase the number of their readers, listeners, and viewers. In the same manner, they do not try to influence the government. By remaining docile, they can count on a maximum degree of governmental cooperation and support. However, if a serious scandal develops, they are obliged to satisfy the public's desire for information. Thus, they must sometimes take bolder and more controversial positions than the government would like. But they usually arrange to do so with great circumspection, so that they actually help the government instead of bringing real pressure on it. Not included here, of course, are those "scandal sheets" that depend for their very existence upon attacks against the government. Generally, they, too, have good reason not to exaggerate their reports in order to avoid any trouble with the authorities. Therefore, they confine their attacks to scandals of secondary importance.

On the other hand, certain other newspapers and news media relegate the profit motive to second place and try to influence the government, public officials, and public opinion. Accordingly, they possess the characteristics of pressure groups. We must distinguish between two types.

Some—such as the newspapers published by unions and corporations—are vehicles of expression for specific groups and cannot be dissociated from them. They are not really distinguishable from the groups whose interests they defend. Thus, there is a whole specialized press, which is nothing more than an outlet for pressure groups. It is interesting to study this type of press, because it provides a very good way of learning about the groups whose views are expressed. Newspapers published by labor unions, employers' associations, and agricultural organizations enable one to become familiar with the activities of these pressure groups. Such publications are usually intended for the members of the group far more than for the general public. They serve a unifying function. Many adopt a characteristic title, calling themselves the "organ" of the group whose views they publish.

However, certain newspapers and news media are intended primarily for the general public, not for the members of the group they represent. Moreover, they sometimes carefully conceal their dependency upon the groups in question and pretend to be independent. Such is the case with what is sometimes called in France *la presse d'industrie*—the press of industry—as opposed to *l'industrie de presse*—the newspaper business—whose purpose is only to sell information. *Industrie de presse* corresponds to the first type we discussed, newspapers of a commercial nature. The *presse d'industrie* consists of newspaper and other news media financed by big industrialists, by banks, and other powerful financial interests that seek to influence the public and the government rather than to make money. The contributors agree to take a loss, or at least to settle for a smaller profit, in order to wield political influence. The newspaper *Le Temps,* purchased by the *Comité des Forges* (the Iron and Steel Committee) in 1929 and financed by it until 1939, was a good example of this very prevalent practice. Many newspapers in the West occupy a similar position. But most of the time, they are simultaneously *industrie de presse* and *presse d'industrie*—which is to say that their owners and publishers endeavor to make money, or at least not to lose any, while they attempt at the same time to influence public opinion and government policies.

A third type of newspaper and information media is provided by independent organizations that seek to exercise a

sort of moral authority over the government and the public—
for example, *Le Monde* in France and a large number of
weekly journals and publications. Accordingly, they constitute
pressure groups somewhat like universities, intellectual circles,
and study groups. They can do so, however, only by maintaining a certain degree of solvency in their enterprises; otherwise, they would be doomed to extinction. Only a few reviews
or weeklies, with a very limited circulation, could survive
under a patronage system provided by a handful of disinterested, wealthy individuals or independent agencies. Large
newspapers could not do so. But experience has shown that if
independent newspapers exist, it is possible to keep them
going (the case of *Le Monde* is typical). The greatest problem
is to create news organs of this type.

THE ORGANIZATION
OF PRESSURE GROUPS

We will examine first the internal structure of pressure
groups and their relationships to political parties, and then,
their methods of operation.

THE STRUCTURE OF PRESSURE GROUPS

We can carry over into the study of pressure groups some of
the distinctions we made with respect to the structure of political parties, especially that of traditional or elitist parties and
mass parties. Moreover, many pressure groups are tied in one
way or another to political parties. The nature of the structural relationships between parties and pressure groups is very
important and enables us to understand each type of organization better.

Mass and Traditional Pressure Groups The distinction between mass pressure groups and traditional pressure groups is

largely based on the distinction between traditional political parties and mass parties, the former being more heterogeneous.

Like the mass parties, mass pressure groups try to incorporate the largest possible membership, since the size of the group is its principal source of strength. As with mass political parties, the inclusion of thousands, even millions, of people requires the establishment of a strong, hierarchical organization. Labor unions exemplify the mass pressure group, after which many other groups have modeled themselves—agricultural organizations, associations of craftsmen, or small businessmen. But we also find mass pressure groups outside the domain of labor unions and corporate enterprises—youth movements, veterans' organizations, feminist organizations, cultural societies, and athletic associations. The communists call groups of this kind, which parallel the political parties, "organizations of the masses."

The technique of mass pressure groups, like that of mass parties, is tied to the idea of organizing large segments of the population. It was first developed in connection with labor unions, along the lines of socialist parties. Accordingly, the development of the working class provided the basis for mass organizations, both the political parties and the pressure groups. These were subsequently imitated by farm organizations and by organizations of the middle classes. Specialized groups—youth, women, veterans, athletes, and so forth—appeared later. At the present time, there is a tendency to develop mass political organizations that are directed, like political parties, to all social categories, but have a single objective, for example, disarmament, and outlawing the atomic bomb (The Peace Movement), the struggle against racism, and propaganda for the European Community. In this way, it is possible to organize people who are reluctant to join a political party, but who feel concern for a particular political or social problem.

In the communist countries of Asia (China and North Vietnam), mass pressure groups are used concurrently with the one-party system to insure a complete organization of the population. Every member of the society is thus caught in a network of interlocking organizations—unions, neighborhood defense groups, youth organizations, women's groups, peace movements, and so on. These "parallel hierarchies" allow for the control and education of the entire population. But even in liberal states, people are also incorporated at times into parallel hierarchies. In Anglo-Saxon and Nordic countries, membership in many different groups—unions, cooperatives, mutual aid societies, civic organizations, veterans' movements, and local groups of various kinds—is very common. The difference is that membership is more or less voluntary, even though it is not formally required in Communist societies, and social pressure can carry a lot of weight in many Western countries. Moreover, by means of parallel hierarchies, many citizens in Western societies take an active part in collective responsibilities.

Like political parties organized through elites, traditional pressure groups do not strive for quantity, but for quality, that is, they address themselves to socially prominent individuals, to the elite. Sometimes organizing on a restricted basis is the result of a deliberate choice; it is deemed preferable to approach certain groups or individuals rather than the general public, because such a strategy seems more likely to achieve the desired goal. This was the attitude among the earlier, traditional parties. Among the earliest elite pressure groups were the intellectual societies of the eighteenth century and the present-day political clubs in France, which bear a strong resemblance to the gatherings of eighteenth century philosophes. The Jean Moulin Club, for example, has only 500 members, but their social status (high government officials, engineers, university professors, and influential journalists) as well as their recognized expertise give the club considerable importance and influence. Larger organizations, like Free Masonry before 1914, exerted great political influence.

Other pressure groups have been obliged to adopt the structure of elite groups by the very nature of the audience they aim to reach. Employers' associations in the iron and steel industry or in the chemical industry can include only a few people of social prominence because such is the nature of the professions they seek to organize. This is also true of every corporative organization in industry, of every association of top administrative officials, of higher education associations, and so forth. In the same category we find associations of writers, poets, and artists, whose political action is very important in certain cases, such as in the Soviet Union today on the question of "liberalization." Last, we can include in this category of elite pressure groups, information offices, and newspaper and information media in general, to the extent that they can be regarded as pressure groups.

The Relations between Political Parties and Pressure Groups

Many pressure groups have no connections with political parties. Others have occasional relations during an election or a strike. Still others have an organic relationship with political parties, which is to say, there are permanent structural ties between the party and the pressure group. There are three possible relationships: (1) some pressure groups are more or less subordinate to the parties; (2) some parties are more or less subordinate to pressure groups; and (3) there are cases of equality between pressure groups in the pursuit of common objectives.

□ PRESSURE GROUPS SUBORDINATE TO POLITICAL PARTIES Socialist parties, and then communist parties, developed the technique for forming "auxiliary organizations," which are actually pressure groups closely tied to a political party and, in fact, subject to its directives. The commonest are youth groups and women's organizations, but there are many others—artistic, literary, and athletic associations; committees for community action; veterans' organizations; mutual aid societies and cooperatives. Sometimes the organic ties to the political party and the dependency on it are officially recognized, as is generally true of youth groups and women's organizations (Socialist Youth, Communist Youth, Socialist Women, Communist Women, and so on). This fact, however, does not prevent tensions from arising between the auxiliary group and the party. Conflicts between political parties and their youth organizations, particularly student organizations, are frequent in all parties and in all countries.

Sometimes a group's dependency and its close affiliation with a political party are not openly acknowledged. The relationship may even be more or less denied. The auxiliary organizations acquire the appearance of independent pressure groups. The party's most common technique for maintaining control is through infiltration, with key positions at all organizational levels being filled by party members, controlled by the party, and subject to party discipline. To preserve a façade of independence, the party sometimes places well-known but ineffectual individuals at the head of the group, giving them honorific titles and functions without any real power. The inclusion of bishops, academicians, and army generals by the Communist party in the [French] National Front of 1944, and in other organizations of a similar nature, was particularly notable in this respect. Often, by keeping the general secretariat, the treasury, and the local secretariats in its hands, the party can control the entire apparatus.

Of course, there are intermediate types between the independent pressure group and the subservient auxiliary groups of a political party. Of special interest is the case of the labor unions. In France and Italy, where they refused any formal collaboration with the socialist parties, the unions eventually fell more or less under their influence. In the 1950's, it was possible to describe the largest French labor union, the CGT [*Confédération Générale du Travail*] as an auxiliary branch of the Communist party—so great was its dependency despite the lack of any organic ties with the party. Today, the situation is more complex. Although the CGT is not entirely independent of the party, it can no longer be regarded as a "transmission belt" for party directives. The union is beginning to enjoy a greater degree of independence in making policy decisions. For its part, the *Force Ouvrière* [another labor union] is rather closely tied to the French Socialist party (the SFIO).

□ POLITICAL PARTIES SUBORDINATE TO PRESSURE GROUPS This is the very opposite of the preceding situation: a political party is subordinate to a pressure group to the extent that it becomes an auxiliary arm of the latter, a situation comparable to that of indirect parties. The British Labour party is typical. Until 1927, when direct party membership began to develop, the party consisted only of representatives of unions, cooperatives, mutual societies, and socialist organizations. It was simply an organization permitting pressure groups to cooperate in the political domain. Since 1927, the party has had an independent existence, apart from the pressure groups who belong to it, because there is now an independent party membership. However, the committees that direct party policies are dominated by union representatives, assuring the latter effective control of the party apparatus. Only a strong leader can counterbalance their influence to some extent. Although the party is not simply an "auxiliary organization" of the pressure groups, it is so to a large degree. The Austrian Popular party (Christian Democratic), which depends entirely on pressure groups—chambers of commerce, farm organizations, and labor unions—is a similar situation.

In all of the foregoing cases, the organic dependency of the party upon the groups that comprise it is officially acknowledged; it is written into the party statutes. But certain conservative parties, which are in fact auxiliary organizations of employers' pressure groups, conceal or disavow their dependency. The great conservative parties of Britain, Germany, and Italy are too powerful to be placed in this category. Moreover, they take pains to establish an organization based on a broad membership in order to offset the influence of powerful economic groups and wealthy party contributors. Weaker and less well-organized parties, like the French Independents, are in a different situation. There are some who argue that if the political right has no solid organization in France, it has no need for it because its true organization and discipline come from the associations of employers that dominate it. It would seem that this view is exaggerated; yet in many countries of Latin America, conservative parties are nothing more than auxiliary organisms for industrial pressure groups and large landowners.

☐ COOPERATION ON AN EQUAL BASIS Mutual cooperation between political parties and pressure groups is encountered, first of all, in special circumstances when parties and pressure groups arrange to cooperate for a time in order to present a united front on a specific issue. We could cite as an example the organizations created by parties and groups of the left to lead the campaign against Leopold III of Belgium following the Second World War; the Resistance groups of 1940–49, some of which continued to operate for a while after the Liberation; committees formed to oppose the OAS [Secret Army Organization] and the "ultras" in France between 1960 and 1962. And in the United States, labor unions have cooperated with the Democratic party during certain elections. Similar phenomena have occurred in other countries. A number of French clubs and civic organizations collaborated with the SFIO in the "Horizon 80" committees which endorsed the candidacy of Gaston Defferre in 1964–65.

Permanent cooperation of a political party and pressure groups occurs in the Scandinavian countries between the Socialist party, labor unions, mutual aid societies, and cooperatives. The unions are not subordinate to the party, nor the party to the unions; they collaborate very closely with one another. A similar situation existed in the Belgian Socialist party before 1940. And, in France, the "Democratic Socialist

Federation," proposed by Gaston Defferre in the spring of 1965 and set up in the fall of that year, thanks to François Mitterand, also established collaboration between parties, clubs, and civic organizations.

PRESSURE GROUPS: THEIR METHODS OF ACTION

We cannot separate the internal structure of pressure groups from the means they use externally, for the latter depend on the former. Mass pressure groups do not act the same as elite groups, and groups that are independent of political parties do not act the same as auxiliary groups.

Pressure groups act on two different levels. On the one hand, they exert direct pressure on government organs—cabinet ministers, members of parliament; and high administrative officials. On the other hand, they exert indirect pressure on the populace to produce a public attitude that will, in turn, influence government leaders, who are always attentive to public opinion.

Direct Action at the Level of Power This is what people think of when they talk about pressure groups—of action taken in legislative corridors and cloakrooms, that is, *lobbying*. But the techniques of direct action at this level are actually much more complex and varied than that.

□ OPEN ACTIONS AND CONCEALED ACTIONS We must distinguish between two kinds of activity at the level of power: one is activity that is open, acknowledged, and sometimes even public; the other is activity that is more discreet, more carefully concealed. Open action includes, first of all, a demand for the fulfillment of promises made by candidates to pressure groups during election campaigns. In 1951, commitments to groups defending private schools [in France] during the controversy over state subsidies played an important role in the political decisions taken by the legislature from 1951 to 1956. The establishment of interparty pressure groups within parliament (groups for the protection of alcoholic beverages, of wine growing, and so forth) and of private associations among legislators (such as the Parliamentary Association for Academic Freedom) also appears to be very effective. The writing of threatening letters to deputies on the eve of important debates may or may not prove influential. Some deputies have, on occasion, denounced and rejected this tactic, which, nevertheless, persists. Finally, sending delegations to parliamentary groups, to government commissions, and to ministers of state represents the most open, the most public, manner of exerting pressure at the level of power.

Discreet action consists, first of all, in financing elections and giving material aid to political parties. This is a very important element in Western democracies, where money retains an enormous influence, but an element that is virtually impossible to study. Less secret, although still discreet, are the personal contacts with legislators and cabinet ministers, or approaches to the heads of governmental agencies—all of which comprises, properly speaking, the activities of lobbies. In France, there is no officially organized lobbying, but unofficial lobbying is quite active and undoubtedly very effective.

☐ FROM CORRUPTION TO INFORMATION In recent years, the activity of pressure groups at the level of power has changed significantly—a change that can be summed up broadly as, "From corruption to information." In its early phase, corruption plays an important role in many varied and often subtle forms. Direct corruption, the outright buying of votes and consciences, is rarer than the public believes. Most politicians are honest—as honest, at least, as businessmen and industrialists—but there are disguised forms of semicorruption, ranging from dinner invitations, expense-paid trips and vacations, to gifts of varying value and importance. Simply forming an acquaintance with men in power, during frequent public receptions, gives one a certain influence on them without in any way impugning their integrity. Above all, collective corruption in the financing of political parties and elections is extremely important.

The methods of exerting pressure have by no means disappeared. Indeed, the development of public relations has tended to perfect this particular semicorruption. But at the same time, another kind of pressure technique has been constantly growing, namely, that of information. A legislator who wants to be well informed about an industrial problem can become so only if the industries involved provide him with the necessary information and documentation. The industries will gladly oblige and skillfully present primarily those facts and opinions favorable to their own interests. Government officials, senators, and deputies thus receive a stream of information from various groups that is important but slanted. Government agencies can, of course, evaluate and reassess this material, which accounts for the growing importance of information made available to those responsible for the formulation of government policies. Despite all this, it must not be forgotten that collective corruption through the financing of parties and election campaigns remains a basic weapon in the arsenal of certain pressure groups. Any political scientist who would deny this fact would be as ludicrous as a biologist who believes that babies are born in cabbages or are brought by the stork.

Indirect Action on the Public Level   In every regime, political power is concerned with public opinion. This is especially true of democracies where those in power must regularly face the challenge of an election and the verdict of the voters. Consequently, by acting to influence public opinion, one can indirectly influence the government. Pressure groups do so in two ways: by propaganda on the one hand, and by violence on the other.

☐ PRESSURE GROUP PROPAGANDA Pressure groups distribute news and information that is slanted, not only to the top levels of government, in the form of carefully researched reports and analyses, but also to the public, in the form of propaganda. This distillation is accomplished in two ways. In the first place, mass pressure groups exert pressure on their own members, this is a very effective means in large mass organizations, such as labor unions, farm organizations, and small businessmen's associations. It is easier to spread the word from the group to the membership, if the latter feel a strong sense of solidarity among themselves and if they have confidence in the leadership of their organization. In France today, organization by pressure groups is far more important than organization by political parties.

Every pressure group, whether a mass or elite group, can make direct propaganda appeals to the public by means of posters, publicity, and advertising campaigns. In the United States, it is common practice for pressure groups to purchase newspaper advertisements, setting forth their point of view; in France, this practice is still frowned upon. However, the procedure is more honest than the undercover action of pressure groups on newspapers that are more or less obedient to their demands. In this domain, the influence of financial and industrial groups on the press remains very significant in Western democracies. In France, the gradual disappearance of the "Resistance press" and control of newspapers by large, private financial interests have had extremely important consequences for political developments of the past twenty years. In 1944–45, newspapers depended on parties, political groups, and independent agencies, but not on special economic interests. Twenty years later, many Parisian daily papers have again fallen under the influence of financial interests. However, the current tendency of the press to become an independent industry helps offset the actions of pressure groups to some extent.

□ THE METHODS OF VIOLENCE An effort to seize power by force is not one of the normal methods used by pressure groups. Rather, it is associated either with a revolution or a *coup d'état*. To be sure, certain groups may take part in such an enterprise. On the other hand, some forms of violence develop as part of the normal activity of pressure groups in their efforts to impress public opinion and, at the same time, force the government to yield to their demands by creating intolerable situations. The technique has been effectively employed by labor unions: general strikes are similar (although they are also intended to bring pressure upon employers). Other groups have adopted these methods, but placed the emphasis on their disruptive features. We have witnessed farm groups blocking public highways, bands of small businessmen in the Poujade movement interfering with government efforts to collect taxes, and winegrowers in the south staging administrative or electoral strikes. Of course, only pressure groups for very large organizations can effectively use such methods, although they may also be used successfully by smaller groups that are strategically situated (for example, the pilots of commercial airlines or elevator operators in New York City skyscrapers).

BIBLIOGRAPHY

Concerning pressure groups in general, consult first the works of J. Meynaud, *Les groupes de pression en France,* 1958; *Nouvelles études sur les groupes de pression en France,* 1962, and his shorter study, *Les groupes de pression,* 1960. These works aim to establish general frames of reference for the study of pressure groups; see also Meynaud's *Les groupes de pression internationaux,* 1961. An important comparative study is W. Ehrmann, *Interest Groups on Four Continents,* Pittsburgh, 1958. Generally speaking, comparative studies are rare.

□ 4 □

THE DIFFERENT KINDS
OF PRESSURE GROUPS

Pressure groups are so numerous and so varied that it is impossible to draw up a list of them for Western Europe, as we were able to do for the political parties. We will describe briefly the principal ones functioning in France and limit ourselves to a few comparative observations about pressure groups in other European countries. For this description we will adopt a classification that is not scientific, but one that has great practical value; we will make a distinction between professional groups—labor unions, employers' associations, farm organizations—and all other pressure groups. Professional groups normally play a greater role than any of the other pressure groups. After the parties, they are the most important political organizations. Except on rare occasions, the political action of other pressure groups is much more limited.

PROFESSIONAL ORGANIZATIONS

By professional organizations, we mean groups that unite people according to their economic activity, which corresponds, as a rule, to the profession they practice. We have indicated the importance of economic phenomena in political life, a condition that holds true on the individual as well as the collective plane. A person's professional activity is an important factor in determining his political attitudes and his participation in political life. This explains why professional organizations play a much greater role than all other types of pressure groups.

EMPLOYERS' ASSOCIATIONS IN BUSINESS AND INDUSTRY

Employers' associations in business and industry, and in related professions like banking, international trade, and insurance, clearly exist only in capitalist countries, even though they have their counterparts in socialist countries. For example, the directors of nationalized industries may form groups to examine their common problems, and then bring pressure on the state to secure more freedom of action within the framework of the government program, more decentralization, and so forth. In such cases, we are dealing with a public pressure group. Be that as it may, we will confine ourselves here to the study of employers' organization in capitalist societies.

We could, however, include organizations of the liberal professions in the same category, some of which are very important. In the United States, for example, medical societies have effectively worked to forestall the development of social security; in France and Belgium, they have tried to delay its implementation; and corporate organizations of the legal profession in France have prevented the modernization of the judiciary and court procedures.

Employers' Organizations in Commerce and Industry In this section, we will describe the French organizations briefly and then make a few remarks about other European organizations for purposes of comparison.

☐ FRENCH ORGANIZATIONS French employers' associations, which were weak before 1939, profited from the experience of the Vichy government. The Vichy regime's "Organization Committees" have disappeared, but the habit of cooperation among employers has continued. Employer groups are much stronger today than they were before the Second World War.

The principal organization is the National Council of French Employers (CNPF), an organization that theoretically includes all employers. But it is a group that is superimposed on other groups. Employers do not belong directly to the CNPF. They belong to the federations (based on branches of production) or to unions (regional in nature), which are themselves members of the CNPF. The CNPF's claim to represent all employers, whose interests are often divergent, weakens the effectiveness of its pressure. It must often adopt a middle-of-the-road position in order to satisfy the majority of its members. However, on many points—salaries and financial policies —it has little trouble obtaining unanimous approval. In the last few years, it seems that, within the council, the federations representing large industries have grown in influence. In any case, certain federations are very powerful, especially those representing a few, highly concentrated firms (the iron and steel and chemical industries, for example). Within the CNPF, business enterprises have a separate and independent organization. A National Business Council includes the professional federations, regional joint-federations, and local groups of small or modest-sized businesses. But the National Business Council is itself too vast; the most effective pressure is often accomplished at the level of its large federations.

Other organizations represent the smaller business concerns and are generally controlled by businessmen. Before 1939, the

Confédération Générale du Patronat Français, forerunner of the CNPF, was made up mostly of large business concerns. Today, despite the CNPF's efforts to attract small business enterprises, the latter remain outside its fold. Their numbers, which give them considerable electoral importance, enable them to indulge in rather brutal pressure tactics, often crude and flamboyant. Until 1952, their principal organization was the *Confédération Générale des Petites et Moyennes Entreprises* (PME), founded by Léon Gingembre. Beginning in 1952, Pierre Poujade's *Union de Défense des Artisans et Commerçants* (UDCA) developed largely at the expense of Mr. Gingembre and the PME. Apparently, the UDCA has had its principal success among small businessmen, while the PME has been more successful in maintaining its hold on the medium-sized business concerns. Since 1957, the Poujade movement has been waning and the PME seems to be recovering its influence. It is noteworthy that in the small and medium-sized enterprises, certain specialized groups are very powerful (truck drivers, for instance).

□ OTHER EUROPEAN ORGANIZATIONS In other European countries, the structure of owner and management groups is somewhat different. In general, industrial enterprises are in a class by themselves, and their organization is the most powerful of all employer groups. Two prominent examples are the Federation of British Industries and the very powerful Federation of German Industries (*Bundesverband der deutschen Industrie*), dominated by the huge iron and steel industry, which provides financial aid to political parties, especially at election time. The almost symbiotic relationship established in Germany between industrial leaders and government circles gives the federation a moral influence and considerable prestige. It publishes and distributes information designed to influence public opinion. On the eve of the 1957 elections, for example, it brought out a brochure which tried to prove that socialist governments have always been beset by economic and social difficulties and have always been opposed to industrial expansion, an absurd allegation, which the example of the Scandinavian countries refutes. The fees the Federation of German Industries collects from its members are very important and provide it with powerful means of action. A collection taken in 1932 in the coal mining cartel of the Ruhr salvaged the National Socialist (Nazi) party.

Alongside these groups dominated by heavy industry, we find more broadly representative organizations of the CNPF type in which the smaller entrepreneurs are generally more powerful: for example, the National Union of Business Leaders in Great Britain, and the Confederation of German Unions of Employers in the Federal Republic. This last group is particularly concerned with the relationship between management and salaried workers' unions. In 1956, it asked all branches of industry to set up a "solidarity fund," primarily intended, it seems, for use in combating strikes. This fund totaled 6 million deutsch marks for the Union of Mine Operators in the Ruhr amassed from a five pfennig assessment on each ton of coal for a period of one year. Clearly, this was a genuine corporate tax. Like the French CNPF, the General Confederation of Industry (*Confindustria*) in Italy includes associations of branches of industry and local associations. It does not extend to those engaged in trade and commerce, but it includes many small business enterprises among the 80,000 firms in its membership. However, it appears that large industries wield a great deal of influence in the Italian confederation. As a rule, it supports right-wing parties and conservative tendencies within Christian Democratic ranks.

The Power of Employers' Organizations   Employers' organizations in business and industry are the most powerful of all pressure groups in capitalist industrial societies, for they reflect basic economic forces. Nonetheless, this fact is disputed, and two opposing theories are offered.

In the Marxist view, Western societies are primarily dominated by capitalism, and employers' organizations are its chief manifestation. Consequently, these organizations possess the fundamental power in society, the true masters of the state, transcending the press, the government administration, the legislature, and the cabinet ministers whom they control. They pull the strings of this puppet show, known officially as politics. Only mass parties, labor unions, and a few independent organizations offer them genuine opposition, but these opposition groups are far weaker than the employers and will remain so as long as the economic system is capitalistic. It is interesting that this view corresponds to rather widespread popular notions. The idea that the "power of money" dominates political life is acknowledged in the West among groups far removed from Marxist circles.

Conservatives and liberals support a diametrically opposed thesis. For them, the Marxist description was valid a hundred years ago, under Louis-Philippe or Napoleon III, but is invalid today. The political institutions of democracy are no longer mere formalities; they have become quite real. The greatest power in the West does not belong to organizations of businessmen and employers, nor to capitalistic forces in general. Rather, it is in the hands of large political parties and labor unions, which dominate governments by means of the ballot and the threat of strikes. The more moderate will concede that, at the very most, there is a balance between the political power of the masses and the economic power of capitalists (which is reflected not only in employers' organizations but also in a whole series of other channels—especially in the direct contacts between government and industry and government and banking). The reader will recognize here the theory of the "plurality of decision-making centers."

Above and beyond doctrinaire controversies, a few facts seem certain. The crude picture of a government and a legislature simply being manipulated by employers' associations, like marionettes controlled by strings, does not correspond to reality. Not only do parties and labor unions intervene, but

so do many other elements—technical experts, high administrative officials, and independent newspapers, for example. All
of these influences gives a margin of independence to the
deputies, ministers, and heads of state, allowing them to maneuver among the antagonistic forces. Moreover, even advocates of the theory of the plurality of decision-making centers
do not dispute that capitalist forces are powerful and carry a
lot of weight in certain political areas. When decisions are to
be made concerning some branch of industry, no one denies
that the employer groups in that particular industry have a
great deal of influence, especially if the industry is an important one. On a more general question, one that concerns industrial production (such as taxes and salaries), the influence
of employer groups is still important, but somewhat less decisive. As for the political domain, properly speaking, employer groups are intervening less often and less effectively
than in the past.

However, their influence appears great at critical moments,
for example, during elections. Election campaigns are financed
to a great extent by employers' associations in capitalist countries, which gives employers a definite influence on national
party organizations. In other respects, employer groups have
a variety of means at their disposal, generally discreet and in-
conspicuous, for influencing government policies. If a socialist
government, or one with socialist tendencies, has a reform
program that disturbs management and ownership, the latter
can do a good deal to prevent the government from taking
effective action. This happened in France in 1924 and again
in 1936, and more recently in Great Britain in 1964. There
the opposition was really led by certain financial interests and
the press, but the employers' groups supported their actions.
And such actions are not channeled through official organizations, which are inclined to adopt a disinterested attitude
in their official capacity. Of course, the sociocultural context
has a great influence on the power of employers and industrial
managers. In Germany and the United States, where there is

little or no socialist ideology, big business and private industry are surrounded with popular respect, and employers' associations are accordingly very powerful. In France and Italy,
where capitalism is a much more controversial subject and its
legitimacy is questioned by a large portion of the population,
employers' associations are weaker, but they are probably still
the most powerful pressure groups in those countries.

FARM ORGANIZATIONS

Employers' associations in industry are generally elite pressure groups. Only organizations of the CNPF type or organizations of businessmen and artisans are mass pressure groups.
On the other hand, farm organizations and unions of salaried
employees are all mass groups, except for a few specialized
groups of large landowners or a few unions of professionals
in the higher echelons.

The Various Farm Organizations As we did with employers'
associations in business and industry, we will describe the
French situation first and, thereafter, several points of comparison with other European countries.

□ FRENCH ORGANIZATIONS Like the organizations in business
and industry, those in agriculture owe at least part of their
present strength to the government of Vichy. By creating the
Farmers' Corporation (*Corporation Paysanne*), the Vichy government gave farmers an impetus to organize. At the time of
the liberation in 1944, the Farmers' Corporation was dissolved
and the General Confederation of Agriculture (CGA) was established as its successor. The need to turn to the CGA in
times of scarcity for fertilizer, gasoline, tractor tires, and other
agricultural necessities made the organization very powerful
at first. But it was subsequently torn apart by a struggle between socialist elements (based primarily on cooperatives, mutual aid societies, and rural groups of engineers) and conserva-

tive elements (chiefly the farm operators) and lost all its influence when the conservatives got the upper hand.

At present, the only general farm organization is the National Federation of the Unions of Farm Operators (FNSEA). Unlike the situation in business and industry, the farm population is not divided by the struggle between the small operators and the big ones. In practice, they have established a *modus vivendi*. Small farmers, burdened with their professional tasks, have long since left to the big farm operators the responsibility of representing them and holding the key positions in their professional organizations. In return, the large operators have defended protectionism and the high prices required to preserve the existence of small, backward farms—a policy that has also increased the profit margin of those operating more modern, economically productive farms. However, under the influence of the younger generation, united in the National Center of Young Farmers (CNJA), the agricultural unions are undergoing profound changes. They are beginning to break away from their traditional ties with conservative circles and to envisage new forms of agriculture—cooperatives, the organizing of markets, and agricultural planning. The CNJA now enjoys considerable influence in the National Federation (FNSEA), where its enterprising young leaders are gradually winning power.

Furthermore, certain specialized farm groups are very powerful, especially those concerned with three major crops—wheat, sugar beets, and wine. An accord reached between sugar beet producers and wine growers before the war of 1914 has had an important influence on French politics for many years, and these two groups remain the pillars of the powerful alcohol lobby, which few governments have dared to challenge. In addition to these professionally based groups, we must include such farm organizations as farm bureaus, mutual aid societies, cooperatives, and the Federation of Farm Property. And let us not forget picturesque and influential groups, like the "moonshiners," who intimidate the politicians.

☐ OTHER EUROPEAN ORGANIZATIONS Farm organizations are powerful in northern and central Europe—in Scandinavia, the Netherlands, Belgium, Austria, and Switzerland. We have seen that in Scandinavia the farm population is represented not only by farm organizations but also by political parties. Farmers' associations are a basic component of the Austrian Popular party, along with the Chambers of Commerce and the Christian Labor Unions. Between 1918 and 1939, the Belgian Catholic party reorganized on a similar basis: the Flemish *Boerenbund* (association of farmers) and its Walloon counterpart comprised one of the four social divisions (*standen*) of the party. In Germany, there is no direct connection between a political party and the National Farmers' Union, but the union carries considerable weight in German politics. The government must take into account its influence when negotiating with the Common Market. The organization's newspaper is extremely militant and often makes bold demands.

The Power of Farm Organizations Farm organizations are powerful, especially in relation to the position agriculture holds in industrial societies. In some European countries, the political influence of farm organizations is disproportionate to the importance of the farmers, a fact that requires explanation.

In Great Britain, farm organizations are rather weak because of the longstanding predominance of business and industry in the British economy. In other countries, however, farm organizations are powerful, reflecting the important role of agriculture in national life. A typical example is Austria, where farm organizations constitute one of the major elements in the Popular party. The case of Italy deserves closer scrutiny. Here there are three principal farm organizations—the General Confederation of Agriculture (*Confagricultura*), the National Confederation of Land Cultivators (*Coldiretti*), and the Federation of the Land (*Federterra*). The first includes mainly nonworking landowners; the second and third include working farmers and farm operators, tenant farmers, and farm workers. The most important of the three is the *Coldiretti,* a very large organization, numbering over 1,700,000 families in 1959, and representing nearly 8 million people: membership is by families, which are the basic social unit, with the head of the family as the go-between. It is also a very wealthy organization because its officials control the associations for the distribution of seed, fertilizer, farm machinery, and chemical products that were established by agrarian reform. Moreover, it is closely tied to the Christian Democratic party and is one of its mainstays. The *Federterra* is much weaker (in 1958, in the elections for farm mutual societies, it received 7.8 per cent of the votes, as against 91.3 per cent for the *Coldiretti*). It is connected to the Socialist-Communist unions of the CGIL (General Confederation of Italian Labor). The *Confagricultura* is closer to the employers' associations and to *Confindustria;* like the latter, it generally supports right-wing parties and the conservative tendencies within the Christian Democratic party.

In other European countries, the farm population wields more political influence than its size and contribution to the national economy warrant. This fact is particularly noticeable in Germany and in France. In France, the sharp decline in the farm population since 1945 has not been reflected by any decrease in political influence. The FNSEA retains all its prestige and influence among the legislators, and if the present government is less swayed by its pressure tactics than in the past, it is because the Gaullist regime is more immune than its predecessor to all types of pressure groups. We must note, however, that French farm organizations tend to adopt violent and anarchical methods—blocking highways, invading cities, and cluttering public streets with tons of unsold farm products—reflecting the anguish of a social class threatened by economic change. And though the decline of the farm population is expressed in their style of protests, there has been no apparent change in agricultural influence. Salaried workers in business and industry far outnumber farm workers in both

France and Germany, yet their demands carry far less weight among legislators and government leaders.

The disproportionate power of farm organizations, in comparison to the real weight of their numbers and their share of the national product, is explained by several factors. In the first place, in France, the wide geographical distribution of the farm population throughout the country gives it an important electoral influence in most *départements,* except for those with several large cities. On the other hand, employees in business and industry, and especially industrial workers, are concentrated in a few *départements,* in which their support is decisive for those seeking public office. But elsewhere, their support is less important than that of the farmers. This means that a majority of the deputies require rural support to be elected, whereas only a minority need the backing of industrial workers and salaried employees. This initial disparity is reinforced by inequities in representation. The Senate, which has been called the "Chamber of Agriculture," is the worst; because of an incredible electoral system, an absolute majority of those selecting its members (53 per cent) come from small rural communities of fewer than 1500 inhabitants and comprise less than one quarter of the country's total population. Even in the National Assembly, there is representational inequity: the deputies from rural regions have a far smaller constituency than those from urban areas, so rural voters carry more weight than city dwellers. This phenomenon is found almost everywhere in Europe.

We must add that in certain countries, workers give their support to opposition parties (the Socialist party in Germany and the Communist party in France), while farmers support the ruling parties. It is natural for the government to bestow its favors on those who support it and to pay more attention to their demands than to the demands of their opponents. This probably explains why rural influence is weaker and why salaried workers in business and industry are stronger in Scandinavia, where socialist parties are often in power. In France, moreover, the municipal structure produces a great many mayors and town councillors in the nearly 30,000 small, primarily rural communities. Also the system of departmental representation insures that the General Councils are, with rare exceptions, comprised mainly of people elected by the rural population. Most local political figures depend on the rural vote for election and more or less represent its views. Consequently, farmers have the upper hand in local politics.

Beyond these material considerations, it seems likely that a psychosocial factor must be taken into account. There is a myth about the earth and those attached to it—the notion that they embody superior values which our technological civilization tends to neglect. There was a lawyer in one legislature of the Fourth Republic who had been elected from a district in Paris as a "peasant" deputy. This certainly is indicative of a particular state of mind. Also, we must not forget that only two generations ago, the majority of Frenchmen were farmers, and most present-day city dwellers—or their parents or grandparents—came from rural areas. Reverence for those who till the soil represents a kind of loyalty to one's origins and reflects, perhaps, a bit of nostalgia. Moreover, in the mentality of the political right, the peasantry incarnates noble values and The Good, as opposed to the industrial workers who represent Evil. One should reread the unintentionally humorous works of René Bazin (*Le blé qui lève, La terre qui meurt*) to learn about this mentality. In Germany also, the Soil and the Peasant are idealized by the conservatives. We mentioned elsewhere how important the sociocultural context is for the effective use of propaganda by pressure groups. In order to be successful, organizations representing special interest groups must find a responsive note among the general public. In many countries, especially France, farm organizations have been the beneficiaries of just such a response.

ORGANIZATIONS OF SALARIED WORKERS

Labor unions constitute the most numerous mass pressure groups. They received their name from their historical origin. At the end of the nineteenth and the beginning of the twentieth century, when they were founded, they were made up almost entirely of industrial laborers. They developed as a result of industrialization and the subsequent formation of a proletariat, which found an advocate in the unions as well as in the socialist parties. But nowadays, in highly developed societies, industrial workers are a minority of all salaried employees. The sector of the economy that provides goods and services has become increasingly important and its employees more numerous than factory workers. Moreover, the distinction between the two categories is growing less distinct; workers in automated factories are more like business employees than traditional laborers. The rise in living standards and the greater uniformity in social outlook have tended to produce a broad middle class. In any event, today's so-called labor unions are actually unions of salaried employees.

The Different Organizations of Salaried Workers   As we did for the commercial and industrial employers' organizations and for the farmers' organizations, we will first discuss French labor organizations and then offer some comparative remarks on the other European organizations.

□   ORGANIZATIONS OF SALARIED WORKERS IN FRANCE   These can be classified into general organizations, special organizations for the elite, and organizations of the "middle classes." The last two types go beyond the notion of organizations for salaried workers since they also include self-employed workers and business owners and managers. The first type, the general organization, is the most important, since it corresponds to the notion of "labor union" as the term is currently used.

The unity of the labor force, that old dream of workers'

struggles, has been shattered in France. Three large central organizations split up the salaried workers' unions—the CGT (General Confederation of Labor), the *Force Ouvrière* (Labor Force), and the CFDT (French Democratic Confederation of Labor). Founded in 1895, the CGT, is both the oldest and the most powerful. Each union belongs simultaneously to a regional union (horizontal) and to a federation of industry (vertical); the central organisms of the CGT reflect this dual structure. Although officially independent, the CGT is actually linked in a certain way to the Communist party. However, an important, non-Communist minority exists within its organization. *Force Ouvrière* (whose exact name is "CGT— *Force Ouvrière"*) resulted from a split within the CGT in December 1947. *Force Ouvrière* represented, before the split, the non-Communist tendency of the CGT, and its defection was encouraged by a financial grant from the government and by subsidies from American labor unions. *Force Ouvrière* has found it difficult to dissociate itself from the conditions of its birth. Its unrelenting anticommunism has often led it to neglect the defense of workers' interests. Its strength is primarily among civil service employees.

In 1964, the old CFTC (French Confederation of Christian Workers), founded in 1919, took the name CFDT (French Democratic Confederation of Labor). Before 1939, the CFTC depended primarily on employees' unions (more especially on women employees). It was not aggressive and had little influence. Since the Liberation, young cadres formed by the JOC (Young Christian Workers) have given it a new impetus by moving it toward the left. The CFDT is less reluctant than *Force Ouvrière* to join the CGT in common actions in the interest of the working class. In fact, in January 1966, the CFDT and the CGT took a decisive step in this direction. In recent years, the CFDT appears to have increased its membership more than the other main labor organizations. Its change of name in 1964 has tended to increase its appeal through the elimination of the reference to Christianity. A small minority among the members of the old CFTC has refused to accept the new name and has split off from the CFDT under the old name of CFTC (a legal decision denied them the right to take the old name, but following an appeal, the case is still pending). This small organization resembles somewhat the pre-World War II CFTC in its lack of aggressiveness, its conformity, and its right-wing orientation.

In addition to these general organizations for salaried workers, we find special organizations for elite groups, like technical experts, engineers, and those in the higher salary brackets (department heads and administrators). The elite also form associations that are affiliated with large general confederations. But outside of these larger organizations, there exists a General Confederation of Cadres (the CGC), which has a rather large membership. This is not a very active organization, however, and its reluctance to take any kind of political action makes it ineffective. Its failure is conspicuous in the area of tax reforms which, in the past few years, have placed the heaviest income tax burden on salaried workers. The organization maintains a fairly conservative outlook.

Middle-class associations have only remote connections with these confederations of salaried workers. Their primary aim is to unite in the same organization the traditional middle-class workers—self-employed workers, businessmen, artisans, craftsmen, doctors, lawyers, and so on—and the modern middle-class workers, namely, salaried elite employees. In France, nearly all of these organizations sacrifice the interests of the latter to the former, as their positions on fiscal matters indicate. Their influence appears rather weak.

□ OTHER EUROPEAN ORGANIZATIONS OF SALARIED WORKERS
Italian trade unions resemble French trade unions in one important respect: both are split by the rift between communists and noncommunists. But on this matter the Italian situation remains unique. The General Confederation of Italian Labor (the CGIL), which corresponds to the French CGT,

includes both the communists and the socialists who belonged
to the old PSI of Pietro Nenni. When the PSI broke its political alliance with the communists in 1956, it did not sever
its connections in the labor field. Nor was the labor alliance
broken by the fusion of the PSI with the Social Democratic
party in October 1966. Alongside the CGIL, a second powerful organization was established by the Italian Confederation
of Labor Unions (the CISL). It is closely tied to the Christian
Democratic party, but a number of its officers and members
belong to the Social Democratic party. The CGIL has about
4 million members, the CISL about 2.3 million. In addition
to these two large confederations, there are two smaller
ones—the Italian Labor Union (600,000 members), which includes Social Democrats and members of the Republican party,
and the CISNAL, a labor union with profascist tendencies that
numbers almost 900,000 members, almost entirely from the
south of Italy.

In the rest of Europe, labor is generally united, and most
organizations show socialist tendencies. There are also a few
Christian labor unions, but they are usually very weak. In
Germany the attempt to start a Christian labor movement in
1955 failed completely. Most salaried employees belong to the
powerful Confederation of German Unions (the DGB), an
enormous, well-organized body of more than 6 million members. But the DGB suffers from internal bureaucracy, and it
is not revolutionary, but moderately reformist. It has relatively
little influence in German political life—certainly not com-
mensurate with the size of its membership and the power of
its organization. In Great Britain, the trade unions are much
more powerful, both because of the Labour party, which they
control, and direct action by the unions themselves in the form
of strikes and boycotts. However, the trade unions suffer from
a degree of institutional rigidity, a result of the unusual stability of their leaders (many retain their posts throughout their
lifetime) and also of their influence on the Central Organization of General Workers' Unions, which lacks dynamic poli-

cies and leadership. The situation in Scandinavia resembles that in Britain, although labor's ties with the Socialist party are not quite so close and formal as those linking the trade unions with the British Labour party.

The Influence of Salaried Workers' Organizations Organizations of salaried workers are powerful and their political influence is important. However, their power and influence are in reality less significant than they are in appearance. Although impressive for the size of their membership, for the means of action they have at their disposal, and for the memories of their revolutionary struggles in the nineteenth century, their influence in Western nations is not as great as the public is inclined to believe.

To measure the influence of labor organizations on political life, it is necessary to analyze the means of pressure available to them. First, they can use the very substantial electoral and political weight of their membership (several millions within the English, German, and Italian unions), a particularly effective tactic for farm organizations and some other pressure groups such as veterans' organizations. It is less effective for unions of salaried employees because their members are usually concentrated in a few urban centers rather than spread over the entire country, as is the farm population. To be sure, their influence is very great in those districts where success at the polls depends largely on the union vote, but there are not many districts of this sort in each country. The electoral weight of 2 million workers is not comparable to the electoral weight of 2 million farmers. Moreover, in Germany with the DGB, and in France and Italy with the unions under Communist influence, organizations of salaried workers support the opposition parties; the parties in power are therefore less responsive to their demands. In Great Britain and in northern Europe, pressure from labor unions is more effective when the governments are socialist.

The second pressure tactic available to labor unions is the

strike, which is no longer simply a weapon to be used against employers. In Western Europe, it is used as a weapon against the government. The strategy is to disrupt the country's economic life, for which the citizens will blame the government, and the government will then be obliged to yield to at least some of the strikers' demands. But this is a double-edged weapon. If the dislocation caused by the strike is attributed by the public to the strikers, and not to the government, the labor unions turn popular resentment against themselves. We have noted how important the social context in which pressure groups operate is to the success or failure of their actions. In strikes called by labor organizations, this context is often uncertain. The conservative element in public opinion is naturally hostile to unions, detesting strikes and any movements that cause disorder and because the popular press often supports this attitude, the government receives support in its effort to turn public opinion against the strikers.

Finally, the influence of salaried workers' organizations varies greatly according to time and place. Generally speaking with respect to Europe, their influence is strongest in Great Britain and Scandinavia where labor unions are very powerful, where they are tied to large political parties that are often in power, and where they do not have a revolutionary character that frightens the public. Their influence appears weakest in the German Federal Republic despite the enormous material strength of the DGB, because public opinion is very conservative, strongly attached to capitalist values, unsympathetic to labor organizations, and naturally hostile to anything that appears to threaten the status quo. Strikes offend most German citizens, which of course greatly diminishes their influence. In France and Italy, the situation is an intermediate one. The fact that the largest labor unions are communist-dominated and therefore appear revolutionary obviously weakens their influence. But on the other hand, capitalism is not as highly regarded in these countries as it is in Germany or the United States, and union resistance to employers and the government appears normal. Then too, certain conservatives believe that granting the workers' material demands will induce them to turn away from communism. This policy sometimes produces at least a partial understanding of the workers' grievances.

Moreover, public opinion on the question of union demands has been undergoing significant change. Formerly, salaried workers in the higher income jobs generally supported government and management whenever factory workers or white-collar workers went on strike. In recent years, however, they have supported the workers' more often, which suggests a growing awareness of a solidarity among all salaried employees. But this trend must not be overestimated. More important is the change in Catholic circles, especially among the church hierarchy. Thirty years ago, when the Archbishop of Lille, Monsignor Liénart, supported the strikers against the owners and managers, most Catholics opposed him. His was an isolated stand, the clergy as a whole favoring the employers. Today the situation is reversed, with priests and bishops more frequently taking up the cudgels on behalf of the strikers. Church collections are sometimes taken to assist their cause. In France and Italy, this has helped to win over a portion of public opinion previously hostile to labor organizations.

OTHER PRESSURE GROUPS

We will describe very briefly pressure groups that are not professional organizations, for they are altogether too numerous and too varied even to be counted. We must not forget that any group or association can exercise some degree of political pressure at certain times and in certain domains, even if it is normally far removed from politics, as, for instance, an athletic club, a church, or the French Academy. A distinction between exclusive pressure groups and partial pressure groups is useful here to establish some order in an area that is so confused and complex. The distinction primarily concerns private groups, which must first be distinguished from public groups.

PRIVATE PRESSURE GROUPS

Most associations and private groups, other than professional organizations, are partial pressure groups—which is to say that political pressure is only part of their activity, and often a very minor part. The groups that are primarily concerned with pressure activity ("exclusive groups") are rare, but they clearly deserve to be examined more carefully than the others.

Exclusive Groups Three main types of exclusive pressure groups are identifiable: specialized political organizations, intellectual societies, and technical pressure groups. We will examine here only the first two, since we discussed the technical groups in the previous chapter.

□ SPECIALIZED POLITICAL ORGANIZATIONS Under this heading are included organizations founded and directed toward a specific political objective, such as outlawing the use of the atom bomb, disarmament, the preservation of world peace, fighting racism, the recognition of a certain boundary or territory, agrarian reform, subsidies for private schools, and election reforms. The pursuit of a single goal is the organization's exclusive concern, and all of its activity consists in bringing pressure on the government, either directly or by means of propaganda designed to influence public opinion. Some of these groups are tied in one way or another to certain political parties, but many are independent. A few have devised fairly original tactics: in France, the Parliamentary Association for Educational Freedom has united, around a group of nonparliamentary activists, deputies and senators favoring government aid for private schools, who thus benefit from the good will of Catholic voters. This group played an important role in educational legislation enacted in 1951 and 1959. In recent years, pacifist organizations and antiracist groups have developed techniques of nonviolence. Their members demonstrate peacefully in the streets without reacting in kind to police brutality. Their opposition consists in passive resistance and physical inertia. In prison, they sometimes resort to hunger strikes. This particular technique requires great courage and sometimes achieves important results because governments fear the reaction of public opinion if people who express their views in this manner are allowed to die. The hunger strike of Louis Lecoin helped the passage of the French law legalizing conscientious objection in 1964.

Two types of specialized political organizations are quite important at the present time: European unity movements and antiracist movements. The former, very prominent during the last fifteen years, have imbued the public with a European ideology which indirectly influences the various European governments. They have not hesitated to bring direct pressure on newspapers, political parties, legislators, and government leaders. Through their actions, they have created a solidarity among politicians of different parties, as, for example, in France, Guy Mollet and certain Socialists, the leaders of the MRP, Maurice Faure and certain prominent Radical politicians, many leaders of the Independent party and so forth. Many political combinations during the Fourth and Fifth Republic have been motivated by this European lobby. Jean Monnet, the leading advocate of the European idea in France, has played a very significant role in both French and European politics. During the last years of the Fourth Republic, General de Gaulle described him as the movement's *inspirateur*.

Antiracist movements have some degree of importance in Europe, especially in the form of anti-Semitic leagues. But they are much more important in the United States, where they play a great role in the struggle by Negroes to obtain equal rights, generally employing nonviolent tactics. In certain southern states, they encounter extreme violence on the part of white supremacists, who are supported by local authorities wielding exceptional power under a federal system with states' rights. Numerous acts of violence in recent years, and several assassinations, have consequently gone unpunished even though the guilty parties were given a courtroom trial and their crimes were patently obvious. Confronted by antiracist groups, racist organizations like the Ku Klux Klan lead the struggle in certain states to maintain segregation and racial inequality.

□ INTELLECTUAL GROUPS   In the eighteenth century, the philosophical and intellectual groups that formulated the doctrines of the French Revolution and prepared the way for that social upheaval were called *sociétés de pensées* [literally, "societies of thoughts"]. The expression lends itself to general application, for we find comparable groups in many countries, at many different moments in history. In France, at the beginning of the twentieth century, Free Masonry and the League for the Rights of Man had a similar influence. They sometimes went further in exerting political pressure than the eighteenth-century *sociétés de pensées*. At one time, Free Masonry established dossiers on army officers to indicate which ones were sympathetic to the Republic and which ones were not. The former would be promoted and the latter kept in less important posts. Though the method of using informers to secure such information was ethically questionable, the motivation for the action was not: most French officers at that period were monarchists and many dreamed of overturning the democratic regime by violence.

At present, the *sociétés de pensées* are being revived in the form of political clubs that developed in France toward the end of the Fourth Republic, and especially since the start of the Fifth Republic. Such clubs include government employees, engineers, university professors, journalists, and graduate students, who study political, economic, and social problems together and seek to discover new solutions adapted to the present needs of French society. Thus the clubs try to formulate programs for social action that can be applied by the government, but their members do not take part in elections or in the legislative processes. Clubs are not political parties; they just exert pressure on the parties, the government, and public opinion. They developed because of the inertia and apathy of French political parties, they do what the parties ought to be doing. The club members generally come from the new generations who should have revitalized the leadership of the political parties, but who are unable to do so because the parties have become old machines, involuted and impervious to change.

Partial Pressure Groups These groups do not devote all their activity to political pressure. They have other objectives and are therefore only partly concerned with acting as pressure groups. Such groups are extremely numerous and varied, since any organization at all may become a pressure group at some point. We will simply list the principal categories.

□ VETERANS' ASSOCIATIONS Such groups have a dual character, acting both as organizations defending their interests (pension and retirement benefits) and as ideological groups. In the latter capacity, they generally add their influence to the political right, and often to the extreme right. In Italy and Germany, they played an important part in the birth of fascism. In France, in 1934, they took an active part in the bloody riots of February 6 [an episode in the Stavisky affair].[1] Reserve officers' associations and military clubs generally exert the same kind of influence. During the 1950's, organizations

---

[1] In 1933, a scandal developed linking Stavisky, a financier dealing in false municipal bonds, with several politicians, including a member of the Chautemps government. This provided rightist political groups with an opportunity to denounce the government.

of veterans who fought in Indo-China and in Algeria developed strong pressure tactics oriented to the far right. In the United States, the American Legion is very conservative. The British Legion in Great Britain is slightly less so. However, certain veterans' groups lean in the opposite direction, intervening on the side of the leftists in favor of peace or disarmament. The societies of former Resistance fighters and of former deported persons are generally associated with the left.

☐ YOUTH MOVEMENTS   Youth movements, such as scouting and student associations, also reflect changing attitudes. Before 1939, they were generally oriented toward the right, but since 1945, they have tended to lean in the opposite direction, although it is difficult to generalize about them in this respect. The development in the scouting movements and among student groups is, however, very striking. They usually have little political influence, with the exception of Catholic youth movements (especially the JOC and the JAC), which have played, and continue to play, an important role. Another exception is student associations; the UNEF (National Union of French Students) has transformed the old organizations, agents of colorful, but futile, demonstrations, into a serious and effective movement. It played a definite role during the period of the war in Algeria, but since then, its influence has diminished.

☐ WOMEN'S MOVEMENTS AND FAMILY ORGANIZATIONS   In France, the main movements in this category expand the influence of the Catholic church and give it a source of political pressure. This is especially true of the powerful League for Catholic Action, controlled by the church hierarchy, which participates indirectly in election campaigns. The Women's Civic and Social Union takes a more direct role in elections. Although it describes itself as "nonpolitical," in practice it supports conservative candidates. Communist women's movements and family associations also have considerable importance, particularly the Union of French Women and various leagues of French housewives. Other, less politically militant organizations are influential in the social domain—in combating such problems as urban ghettos and alcoholism. In the United States, the powerful League of Women Voters encourages civic education among women voters and champions legislation favoring equality of the sexes.

□ IDEOLOGICAL AND RELIGIOUS GROUPS Organizations dependent upon the Catholic church are the most powerful in France. The Assembly of Cardinals and Archbishops and the Plenary Assembly of the Episcopate take very general positions. More specific stands are taken by groups of laymen—either general groups, such as Catholic Action or Women's Leagues, or specialized groups, such as the very powerful Association of Pupils' Parents for Educational Freedom (the APEL) or the no-less-powerful Parliamentary Association for Educational Freedom, of which we have already spoken.

Other ideologically important groups depend, in varying degrees, on the university. Teachers' unions, various university committees, and the League for Education exercise a greater moral than material influence, but are by no means ineffective. Although the old League for the Rights of Man, founded during the Dreyfus affair, has fallen from its former exalted position, it still continues to wage courageous battles. Certain intellectual groups, formed under special circumstances, play an important role at particular moments; for example, the National Committee for Public Action in 1959, and various groups of intellectuals concerned with the defense of civil rights in Algeria between 1956 and 1962.

PUBLIC PRESSURE GROUPS

We mentioned earlier that the notion of public pressure groups has been challenged by those who believe that only private organizations really bring pressure on the state; governmental agencies and those providing public services cannot do so because they are the state. But this juridical concept of the state and of the power of government is no longer tenable. The government and the state are themselves a complex organization, and the governmental agencies responsible for making political decisions—parliament and the government—are subject to pressures from certain elements within the state. In this connection, we must distinguish between pressure from civil organizations and pressure from the military.

Pressure from Civil Organizations We can recognize two main types of public pressure groups—government agencies (*administrations publiques*) and civil service cadres (*corps de fonctionnaires*).

☐ GOVERNMENT AGENCIES Although, in principle, government agencies are elements of the state, in practice, the problem in modern states is to prevent each of them from becoming an autonomous, self-serving organization that confuses its own specialized interests with those of the public. The problem is never entirely resolved, and certain administrative agencies therefore resemble pressure groups. We will simply cite two typical examples. The first is that of decentralized public services or nationalized industries with a certain degree of independence. They naturally endeavor to influence the state in much the same way as do large private enterprises. From this standpoint, one could study the tensions and rivalries that exist between state enterprises in socialist societies.

The second example is that of specialized agencies that develop special relationships with certain social or professional groups. Often, such agencies tend to share and reflect the attitudes of these groups and to support their demands upon the government, instead of interpreting and carrying out the government's policies as they are supposed to do. The case of the French Ministry of Agriculture during the Fourth Republic was striking. It supported the farmers' point of view so thoroughly that, in certain finance committees composed of government representatives and representatives of the taxpayers, the ministry's delegates voted with the taxpayers rather than with the other government officials. One might say that the Ministry of Agriculture was at that time the "number one" pressure group for farm interests. It is true that its policies also served as a springboard for certain politicians.

□ CIVIL SERVICE CADRES   Certain groups of civil servants form closely knit associations within the state and exercise considerable influence over government agencies and government policies. The most famous example in France is that of the Bureau of Accounting, the members of which are known for their intelligence and technical and administrative competence. Having developed a strong sense of solidarity among themselves, consequently, they have gradually infiltrated the Ministry of Finance, where they occupy the principal administrative posts. They run many other governmental agencies, and they hold important positions in the ministerial cabinets. However, their role in government must not be exaggerated. They have not formulated any political doctrine or defined any specific objectives that they consciously seek to apply through the positions they occupy. But they share a common education and orientation that leads them unconsciously to guide state policies in the direction dictated by their particular views and attitudes.

We could cite other instances such as the Council of State and the Corps of Mining Engineers. In all of these cases, we are dealing with officially organized administrative bodies. Another type of civil service cadre is made up of the graduates of certain famous schools. Though they do not constitute an administrative body as such, they preserve "old school ties" among themselves and thus become a de facto community. Graduates of the National School of Public Administration play a significant role in a number of public agencies, as do the graduates of the *Ecole Polytechnique* in the French rail-road industry (the SNCF) and other nationalized industries.

The Military as a Pressure Group We have already indicated the political danger posed by the military, which nations are not always successful in protecting themselves against. If the military establishes itself as a pressure group, it can threaten to destroy the state. This extreme situation is frequently realized in Latin American countries and other underdeveloped nations. And France became "South-Americanized" in this way between 1958 and 1962. Occasionally, the military plays the role of a civilian pressure group, but its strength makes it much more disturbing.

☐ INTERVENTION BY FORCE When an army effects a coup d'etat and seizes power itself, it is no longer a pressure group but the state in its own right, that is, a military dictatorship. In the Iberian countries, the army's intervention in politics is often accomplished in a less obvious manner. The military do not take overt control of the government. They select a politician who enjoys their confidence, install him in office, and keep him there. It is then said that the army has spoken, and their action constitutes a *pronunciamiento*. This simply means that the government no longer rests on popular approval, but on the force of arms. The case of Portugal is typical. Salazar was brought to power by the army, which likewise kept him in power. Many Latin American governments are in the same situation. Sometimes military support is not sufficient for seizing power, but it certainly helps, or, at the least, limits the government's freedom of action.

France underwent a comparable phase between 1958 and 1962. The army played a decisive role in bringing about the fall of the Fourth Republic and the establishment of the Fifth. May 13, 1958, was not exactly the occasion for a *pronuncia-miento,* but it bore a striking resemblance to this military type of coup d'etat.[2] Certain officers had adopted a doctrine which they said was drawn from Mao Tse-tung—the doctrine of "subversive warfare"—and they used it to justify the army's intervention in politics. Moreover, army pressure antedated the action of May 13: French officers in Algeria, allied with colonial interest groups, had a great deal of political influence in the last two years of the Fourth Republic. Although the new regime tried to reduce this influence, General de Gaulle's efforts to bring the army back under control were slow to show results. Meanwhile, there was the rebellion of January 24, 1960 (encouraged by elements of the Algerian army), the military *putsch* of April 1961, and the complicity of many of the military in the development of the OAS (Organization of the Secret Army). During the Fifth Republic, the army continued to be one of the principal pressure groups until 1962. Since then, its influence has almost completely disappeared.

☐ POLITICAL PRESSURE   In the more "civilized" (in the literal sense of the word) states, the army does not intervene directly by force. Rather, it exerts a psychological pressure that is all the more powerful for being supported by civil groups and by public opinion. Thus, in Imperial Germany (1871–1914) and during the Weimar Republic (1919–33), the officer corps and the general staff played an extremely important political role. The role of the military has been less powerful in the other industrial nations, but it is rare for the army not to exercise some measure of influence.

The case of the United States deserves a careful analysis,

[2] In 1954, the Algerians rebelled in pursuit of independence from France. Certain French army officers, angered by de Gaulle's promises of future independence, attempted an insurrection in January 1960. De Gaulle, however, successfully retained the allegiance of the French army, began negotiations with Algerian leaders, and started to bring the army home. In a referendum held in July 1962, an overwhelming majority of Algerians voted for independence.

which we cannot give here. The military have a great moral influence there, because of the general fear of a nuclear war and the feeling of security provided by military power. But the military has also acquired considerable material influence. The most important industrial orders are placed by the military services, whose huge defense requirements account for a large part of the nation's economic activity. Many important private firms depend entirely on defense contracts. They have discovered that they secure contracts more readily if they place former officers on their boards of directors—men who are familiar with military procurement methods and who have personal connections with those in key positions in the Defense Department. Such firms have a vested interest in the development of armaments and in the extension of operations of the type undertaken in Vietnam or the Dominican Republic. For their part, the officers believe that such operations are in accord with American interests. This combination of economic interests with the interests of a particular community has produced what President Eisenhower (who was both a conservative and a military man) called the "military-industrial complex"—a situation that poses a grave danger for the future of the United States.

BIBLIOGRAPHY

Concerning pressure groups in Europe, see the aforementioned bibliography of J. Meynaud and J. Meyriat in the *Revue Française de Science Politique,* 1959, p. 229, and 1962, p. 433; W. Ehrmann, *Interest Groups on Four Continents,* Pittsburgh, Pa., and "Les groups d'intérêt et la bureaucratie dans les démocraties occidentales," *Rev. Fr. de Sci. Pol.* (1961), p. 541: R. C. Breever, *European Unity and the Trade Union Movement,* London, 1960; A. Tiano, "L'action des syndicats ouvriers: état des travaux," *Rev. Fr. de Sci. Pol.* (1960). By way of comparison, one can consult L. Dion, *Les groupes de pouvoir politique aux Etats-Unis,* Québec, 1965.

Concerning pressure groups in France, see the two studies by J.

Meynaud, *Les groupes de pression en France,* 1958, and *Nouvelles études sur les groupes de pression,* 1962, and his article on pressure groups under the Fifth Republic, *Rev. Fr. de Sci. Pol.* (1962), p. 672; W. Ehrmann, *La politique du patronat français (1936–1955),* 1959; and the special issue of the journal *Esprit,* June 1953. See also the special issue of the *Revue Française de Science Politique,* December 1959, on "The Intellectuals in Contemporary French Society"; G. Adam, *La C.F.T.C. (1940–1958),* 1964, and *Les elections sociales en France,* 1964 (gives details on the strength of the various labor unions); A. Prost, *La C.G.T. à l'époque du Front populaire,* 1944; J. Fauvet, and H. Mendras, *Les paysans et la politique dans la France contemporaine,* 1958; A. Coutrot and F. Dreyfus, *Les forces religieuses dans la société française,* 1966; A. Latreille, and A. Siegfried, *Les forces religieuses et la vie politique,* 1951; A. Dansette, *Destin du catholicisme français (1926–1956),* 1957; Stuart R. Schram, *Protestantism and Politics in France,* Alençon, 1954; G. E. Lavau, "Note sur un 'pressure group' français: la Confédération générale des Petites et Moyennes entreprises," *Rev. Fr. de Sci. Pol.* (1955), p. 370; H. Mendras, "Les organisations agricoles et la politique" *Rev. Fr. de Sci. Pol.* (1956), p. 736); V. Lorwin, *The French Labor Movement,* Cambridge, Mass., 1954; R. Rémond, "Les anciens combattants et la politique" *Rev. Fr. de Sci. Pol.* (1955), p. 267; and "Droite et gauche dans le catholicisme français contemporain," *ibid.* (1958), pp. 529 and 803.

Concerning pressure groups in Germany, see R. Breitling, *Die Verbünde in der Bundesrepublik,* Meisenham, 1955; the works of K. Pritzkoleit concerning business employers and management: *Männer, Mächte, Monopole,* Düsseldorf, 1953; *Die Neuen Herren.* Vienna and Munich, 1955; *Wem gehört Deutschland,* Vienna and Munich, 1957; concerning labor unions, see G. Triesch, *Die Macht der Funktionäre,* Düsseldorf, 1956, and especially the collective work *Gewerkschaften und Staat,* Düsseldorf, 1956. Concerning pressure groups in Great Britain, see A. Potter, *Organized Groups in British National Politics,* London, 1961; S. E. Finer, *Anonymous Empire: a Study of the Lobby in Great Britain,* London, 1958; J. D. Stewart, *British Pressure Groups,* Oxford, 1958 (examines especially the influence of pressure groups on the House of Commons); P. Steff and H. Storing, *The State and the Farm,* London, 1962; V. L. Allen, *Trade Unions and the Government,* London, 1960: D. F. Mac-

Donald, *The State and the Trade Unions*, London, 1960; H. W. Weiner, *British Labour and Public Ownership*, London, 1960; H. Welton, *The Trade Unions, the Employers, and the State*, London, 1960; Concerning pressure groups in Italy, see J. G. La Palombara, *The Italian Labor Movement*, Ithaca, N.Y., 1957. Concerning pressure groups in Belgium, see W. J. Ganshof Van Der Meersch, *Pouvoir de fait et règle de droit dans le fonctionnement des institutions politiques*, Brussels, 1957; the article by P. Goldschmidt-Clermont on employers' groups in the *Revue de l'Institut de Sociologie Solvay*, 1957, p. 513; L. Delsinne on the labor movement and politics, *ibid.*, 1957, p. 39. Concerning pressure groups in Scandinavia, see G. Heckscher, *Staten och organisationerna*, 2d ed., Stockholm, 1951, and H. Ferraton, *Syndicalisme ouvrier et social démocratie en Norvège*, 1960.

☐ INDEX ☐

159